D0508400

The Magic of QUILTMAKING

A BEGINNER'S GUIDE

Margaret Rolfe and Jenny Bowker

Martingale®
& COMPANY

The Magic of Quiltmaking: A Beginner's Guide
© 2004 by Margaret Rolfe and Jenny Bowker

That Patchwork Place® is an imprint
of Martingale & Company®.

Martingale & Company
20205 144th Avenue NE
Woodinville, WA 98072-8478
www.martingale-pub.com

Credits

President: Nancy J. Martin
CEO: Daniel J. Martin
Publisher: Jane Hamada
Editorial Director: Mary V. Green
Managing Editor: Tina Cook
Technical Editor: Karen Soltys
Copy Editors: Karen Koll, Melissa Bryan
Design Director: Stan Green
Illustrator: Robin Strobel
Cover and Text Designer: Stan Green
Photographers: Brent Kane and Andrew Sikorski

Mission Statement

Dedicated to providing quality products
and service to inspire creativity.

Printed in China
09 08 07 06 05 04   8 7 6 5 4 3 2 1

No part of this product may be reproduced in any form, unless otherwise stated, in which case reproduction is limited to the use of the purchaser. The written instructions, photographs, designs, projects, and patterns are intended for the personal, noncommercial use of the retail purchaser and are under federal copyright laws; they are not to be reproduced by any electronic, mechanical, or other means, including informational storage or retrieval systems, for commercial use. Permission is granted to photocopy patterns for the personal use of the retail purchaser.

The information in this book is presented in good faith, but no warranty is given nor results guaranteed. Since Martingale & Company has no control over choice of materials or procedures, the company assumes no responsibility for the use of this information.

Library of Congress Cataloging-in-Publication Data

Rolfe, Margaret.
    The magic of quiltmaking : a beginner's guide /
Margaret Rolfe and Jenny Bowker.
        p. cm.
    "That Patchwork Place."
    Includes index.
    ISBN 1-56477-502-X
  1. Patchwork—Patterns. 2. Appliqué—Patterns. 3.
Quilting. I. Bowker, Jenny. II. Title.
    TT835 .R65137
    746 .46—dc22
                                        2004003598

Acknowledgments

Margaret and Jenny are indebted to many others for the making of this book. We are grateful to Martingale for backing our vision for the book, especially Mary Green. We thank Andrew Sikorski for his photography and his constant and cheerful commitment to getting it right and getting it done on time. Kathryn Hailey generously made the Pieced Sampler quilt for us, to try out our instructions. Carmel Fardoulis assisted Margaret with some timely hand finishing. Our talented quilting friends helped us very much by generously sharing their special areas of expertise: Beth Miller on hand appliqué, Barbara Goddard on machine appliqué, and Kerry Gavin on hand quilting.

Above all, we thank our families for all their help and encouragement. Margaret is grateful to her daughter-in-law, Janine, for reading parts of the manuscript as a nonquilter, and to her daughter Melinda, for specially visiting to help sew bindings. Margaret's mother, Linda Poppins, and her sister-in-law, Helen Poppins, also helped with bindings. As always, Margaret's husband, Barry, was encouraging and supportive and cheerfully endured many weekends when she was totally preoccupied with sewing and writing.

Jenny is grateful to her daughter, Karmen Hoy, who read parts of the book, made comments, and tied knots to instructions. Her daughter Tabbi was a perfect hand model, and Tabbi and her brother Sam cooked, cleaned, and did all the things Jenny would have been doing if she hadn't been working on the book. Her husband Bob was helpful and encouraging, seeing her preoccupation and absences as a fair and reasonable payback for his Ph.D.

Contents

Introduction

Welcome to the wonderful, magical world of quiltmaking in the twenty-first century!

We call it magic because in recent years, new tools and techniques

have revolutionized a centuries-old craft.

Pieces can be cut out quickly and accurately with rotary cutters, sewing machines can be used for quilting in new ways, and products from other fields, such as spray starch, can be used to make accurate shapes for appliqué.

Quiltmaking is also magical because it is a wonderful world of color and creativity. From your first quilt you will have the pleasure of playing with beautiful fabric that today is produced in a rainbow of colors and myriad designs. Whether little or big, simple or complex, your quilts will always reflect your own creativity because of the unique combination of fabrics you choose to put into them.

The goal of this book is to introduce you to the techniques and concepts of quiltmaking. The major skills and concepts you will be learning are **piecing**, the sewing together of fabric patches; **appliqué**, the sewing of patches onto a background fabric; and **quilting**, the sewing together of the quilt layers (quilt top, batting, and backing fabric). We stress both skills and concepts because we aim not only for you to understand the techniques of quiltmaking, but for you to be able to think like a quiltmaker as well.

Our intent is not to include all the techniques of quiltmaking—that would take a much larger book than this one. Rather, our goal is to give you a sound knowledge of the basics. This knowledge

Pieced Block

Appliqué Block

Quilted Block

will enable you to make any number of quilts from the designs and ideas presented here, and to have the confidence to approach other quilts and patchwork designs. Like the foundations of a house, the information and skills presented in this book will give you a sound basis on which to build new techniques and ideas later.

From our own wide experience of quiltmaking we will share with you the techniques that we find work for us and for our students. We do not claim these are the only ways of doing things, but we are confident they will give you good results.

Indeed, results are what it is all about, and your results will be wonderful quilts!

~ Margaret Rolfe
~ Jenny Bowker

Using This Book

We describe in detail the main processes of piecing, appliqué, quilt assembly, and quilting. We give reasons for what we suggest so that you will understand not only how but also why techniques are performed a certain way. Sometimes we provide exercises that will increase your understanding as well as help you build your skills.

We hope you will then make some of the projects. They have been designed carefully to let you put into practice the techniques and concepts described in this book. The quilts are arranged in a progression from easiest to more complex to help you develop your skills. We strongly recommend that you make them in order, beginning with "Four Patch" on page 96. We hope you will make "Piecing Sampler," which will introduce you to nine different patchwork designs and many different piecing techniques. After this, you may like to try other pieced quilts or continue into appliqué. All quilt instructions are cross-referenced to the general text that describes in detail the processes involved.

At the back of the book you'll find a handy cutting chart for the most commonly used patchwork shapes. Also we've included a comprehensive index so that you can look up words and techniques at any time.

A WORD ABOUT MEASUREMENTS

Quiltmaking is a craft that is now enjoyed worldwide, so our instructions include both imperial and metric measurements. Imperial measurements are given first, followed by metric measurements in brackets. For example, "Cut a square, 4" x 4" [10 cm x 10 cm]." **NOTE:** The metric equivalents are all the nearest practical whole number, so the imperial and metric measurements are not interchangeable. The same measurement may even have different equivalents at different times, depending on how it is derived. Work only in the measurement system familiar to you.

What Is a Quilt?

A quilt is a sandwich of three layers held together by quilting stitches.

- The quilt top is a layer of fabric pieces sewn together by piecing or appliqué; it is also called patchwork.

- The batting is the middle layer of padding.

- The backing is the layer of fabric at the back, or "wrong," side of the quilt.

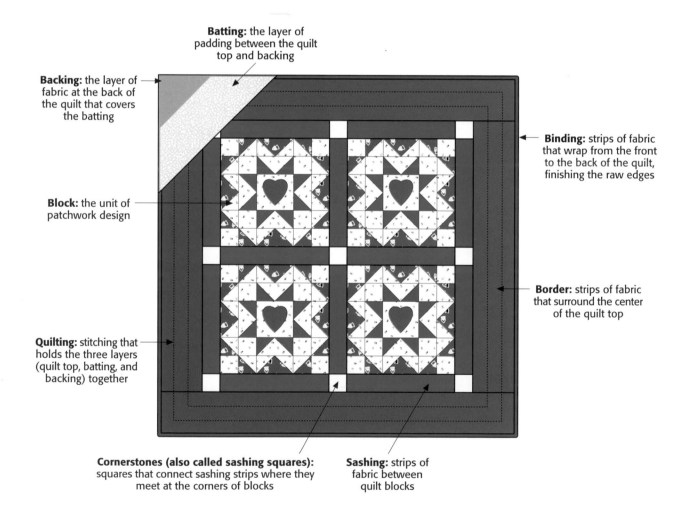

Batting: the layer of padding between the quilt top and backing

Backing: the layer of fabric at the back of the quilt that covers the batting

Binding: strips of fabric that wrap from the front to the back of the quilt, finishing the raw edges

Block: the unit of patchwork design

Border: strips of fabric that surround the center of the quilt top

Quilting: stitching that holds the three layers (quilt top, batting, and backing) together

Cornerstones (also called sashing squares): squares that connect sashing strips where they meet at the corners of blocks

Sashing: strips of fabric between quilt blocks

The block in this quilt combines piecing and appliqué. The piecing consists of patches of fabric joined side by side to make a block design called Eddystone Light. The appliqué consists of a heart-shaped patch of fabric added to the center of the block.

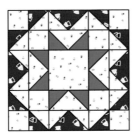

Eddystone Light Block

Pieced Shapes

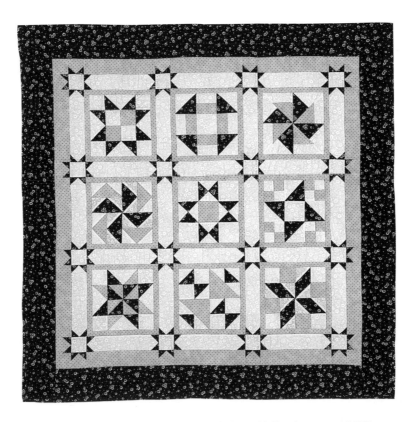

Appliqué Unit

Quilts can include some or all of these possibilities—and every variation of them that you can imagine. There are thousands of different pieced and appliqué block designs, as well as blocks that combine both. Quilts may have multiple borders or no borders. They may have sashing without cornerstones, complex pieced sashing, or no sashing at all. There are also quilts that have no piecing or appliqué, but are simply made from large pieces of fabric; they are called **whole-cloth** quilts. Some quilts have only two layers—a top and a backing with no batting. It's all these possibilities that make quiltmaking so creative and exciting!

Sampler quilts are so named because they contain a variety, or samples, of different block designs.

KATHRYN'S SAMPLER made by Kathryn Hailey (see page 109)

Tools and Equipment

There are some essential tools that you must have to begin making quilts.

Buy quality equipment—it's an investment that will pay off in the long run.

Sewing Machine

Your sewing machine is the most important piece of equipment for making quilts. Take a little time to become acquainted with yours; this time will be amply repaid in happy hours spent sewing.

It is beneficial to understand the important aspects of your machine. Read this section while sitting at your sewing machine, with the manufacturer's instruction book handy to help you identify the parts on your machine.

Tension. The machine sews with two threads, a top one that is threaded from the spool through the needle and a bottom one that is wound onto a small, round bobbin. When the needle goes down, it takes the top thread through the fabrics and makes a loop that goes around the bobbin thread. This action locks the upper thread around the lower thread. If the tension is correct, the threads lock in the center of the fabrics as they are sewn together. Tension of the upper thread can be adjusted by changing the number on the tension dial or tension setting. It is generally best to leave the tension of the bobbin thread to an expert.

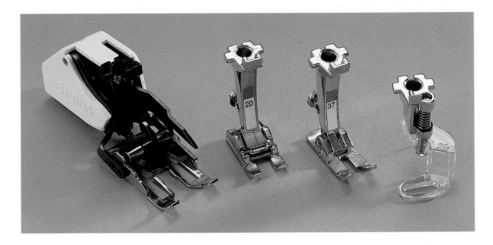

Left to right: Walking foot, embroidery foot, patchwork ¼" foot, free-motion quilting or darning foot. (Note that feet may vary from those shown, depending on the brand.)

Presser foot. This part of the machine surrounds the needle and presses down on the fabrics, keeping them in place for stitching. A lever sets the presser foot in position, either up, so that you can place the fabric under the needle, or down, where it will hold the fabrics in place and be ready for stitching. In addition to the standard presser foot, your machine most likely can accommodate various feet that are suitable for specialized tasks. Several machine feet are especially important for quiltmaking. Purchase those made for your particular machine make and model, as feet vary from machine to machine.

- **Patchwork or ¼" foot.** This foot (applies only for people using imperial measurements) is especially designed for machine piecing so that the side edge of the foot is ¼" from the needle, enabling you to make a consistent ¼" seam by aligning the cut edge of the fabric with the edge of the foot.

- **Walking foot.** Used primarily for machine quilting or attaching binding, this foot adds the equivalent of an extra set of feed dogs coming from above the fabric, helping to move the multiple layers of the quilt through the machine smoothly. In some machines, a walking foot (also called an even-feed foot) is built in and just needs to be engaged.

- **Free-motion quilting or darning foot.** Use this foot for free-motion machine quilting. It releases the pressure on the fabrics between each stitch. This enables you to move the fabrics about freely so you can sew in any direction you choose.

- **Embroidery foot.** Also called an open-toe foot, this presser foot is used for machine appliqué. It has a wide opening at the front of the foot, giving you good visibility for stitching.

Stitch length. The machine makes longer or shorter stitches according to where you set the control for stitch length. A setting of 12 stitches per inch, or 2.5 on electronic machines, is typically used for patchwork.

Feed dogs. These are jagged teeth that come up from beneath the presser foot. The combined action of the presser foot pushing down and the feed dogs moving backward is what moves the fabrics through the machine. For free-motion quilting, the feed dogs are dropped down so the fabric is not moved through the machine.

Throat plate and bed. Around the presser foot, the immediate metal area is called the throat plate, and the wider flat area is called the bed.

Needles. For ordinary piecing and quilting, use size 80/12 universal needles. For machine appliqué, use size 70/10 embroidery needles.

Needles become dull, so it's a good idea to get in the practice of changing the needle on a regular basis. Once you hear the needle thumping through your fabric, it's already past time to change it!

Machines vary, so consult the instruction booklet for precise information about your machine, including how to thread it, wind bobbins, set the tension, and drop the feed dogs. The book should also tell you what presser feet are available for your machine. Pay particular attention to the recommended cleaning and oiling procedures (if your machine requires this), and perform them often.

If you are looking to buy a new machine, ask the demonstrators to show you the sewing that you will be doing as a quiltmaker. Ask them to demonstrate how the machine will make an accurate ¼" [7.5 mm] seam allowance and to show you machine quilting, including free-motion machine quilting with the feed dogs dropped.

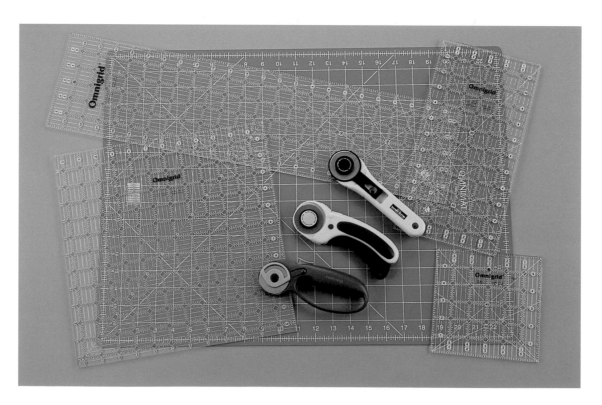

Rotary-cutting equipment: rulers, mat, and choice of cutters

Rotary-Cutting Equipment

Rotary cutter. This is a circular blade mounted on a handle. It cuts cleanly, easily, and exactly by being rolled alongside a ruler. Rotary cutters come in different sizes, but the medium size with a 45 mm-diameter blade is ideal for most situations. There are various styles of cutter handles, so choose the one that suits your hand best.

Cutting mat. Essential to use with the rotary cutter, the mat has a special self-healing surface that can withstand the sharp blade and protect your table surface. Buy the largest mat you have space for. We recommend at least 17½" x 23½" [45 cm x 60 cm].

Rulers. Rulers used for rotary cutting are made of clear acrylic so that the fabric is visible through the ruler. They are thick enough so that you can roll a rotary cutter alongside them with little risk of the blade slipping. They should be clearly printed with a grid of measurements, with ⅛" [5 mm] intervals marked. Look for rulers that include a line indicating the 45° angle.

We recommend you start with three essential rulers: first, a long ruler, 6" x 24" [16 cm x 60 cm], for cutting long strips and borders; second, a short ruler, 6" x 12" [16 cm x 32 cm], for crosscutting strips and cutting smaller shapes; and third, a large, square ruler, 12½" x 12½" [32 cm x 32 cm], for cutting large squares and shapes. These rulers will allow you to do all basic cutting. Another highly desirable size is a 6½" x 6½" [16 cm x 16 cm] square with the diagonal marked, for cutting small shapes. There are lots of special rulers for cutting all kinds of patchwork shapes, but buy the basic ones first. Note that it is not necessary to purchase rulers with exactly these measurements, as some brands may vary a little. We also recommend that you buy some special nonslip film that can be attached to the rulers to prevent them from slipping on the fabric.

Preparing Metric Rulers

As most metric rulers do not have a 7.5 mm mark around the edge, add this line to one side of the 16 cm x 32 cm size. Using an ordinary ruler and a fine-point, permanent marker, measure and mark a line 7.5 mm parallel to the edge of the ruler. Use this line to mark a 7.5 mm seam allowance when required.

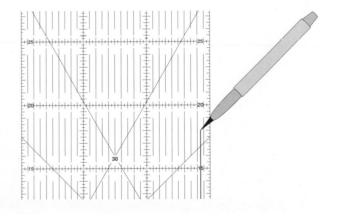

Basic Sewing Supplies

You may well find that you already have much of the basic sewing equipment required for quiltmaking, such as dressmaking scissors and an iron.

Iron

An iron is used continuously for quiltmaking, so set up an ironing station conveniently near your sewing machine. Many irons come with "auto-off" features, meaning they'll automatically turn themselves off if they aren't used for a specified period, such as 10 minutes. As a quilter, you may find this feature to be more of a nuisance than a benefit.

For piecing, use the iron on the steam setting. If you prefer the dry setting, use a plastic spray water bottle to dampen your work when needed. For appliqué, use a dry iron when preparing pieces using spray starch. Finished appliqué blocks may be steam pressed.

Scissors and Seam Ripper

Dressmaking scissors. A pair of shears is useful for cutting fabric and batting. For appliqué, it is helpful to use a sharp pair of scissors with blades about 4" [10 cm] long, but ordinary dressmaking scissors are fine.

Small scissors or thread snips. Keep small scissors or thread snips next to your machine for cutting threads as you sew.

Seam ripper. This small gadget has a narrow blade and a sharp point. It is used to cut thread so you can unpick stitching. All quilters need one, as we all undo seams from time to time. Look for a quality seam ripper with a fine, sharp blade.

Top to bottom: seam ripper, small scissors, dressmaking scissors, and thread snips

Needles and Pins

Needles. Your choice of needle for hand sewing is personal; use what is comfortable in your hand. Note that a larger, fatter needle requires more effort to push it through the fabric, so finer needles are easier to use. If you find it hard to thread a needle, also choose a quality needle threader.

- **Sharps or Crewels.** For hand sewing, which includes hand piecing, appliqué, and attaching bindings, try a size 9 Sharp or Crewel needle. Crewel needles are easier to thread as they have larger eyes.

- **Betweens.** For hand quilting, use a Between needle, a special short needle designed for that purpose. The larger the number, the smaller the needle will be. To begin with, use a size 8, 9, or 10.

- **Darning.** For thread basting, use a long needle such as a Darning needle.

- **Straight pins.** Pins are used to hold fabrics together, to mark lengths of fabric, and to hold appliqué pieces in place. For piecing, ball-head pins are easy to use and hard to lose. For appliqué, use dressmaking pins.

Equipment for Template-Making and Marking

Pencils. Use a medium pencil to draw blocks and mark fabric for hand piecing and hand quilting. Keep points sharp with a sharpener or use a mechanical pencil. Use a silver pencil to mark dark fabrics.

Template plastic. Templates are the pattern shapes used in piecing and appliqué. Template plastic marked with a grid is best for hand-piecing templates.

Graph paper and ruler. These are used to draw blocks. Any sort of ruler can be used.

Fine-point permanent markers. These have lots of uses, including tracing patterns onto template plastic and writing on fabric to make labels for your quilts.

Lightweight card stock or manila folders. Use these to prepare shapes for hand appliqué.

Sandpaper. For hand piecing, use a sheet of fine sandpaper to grip the fabric while you are marking around templates.

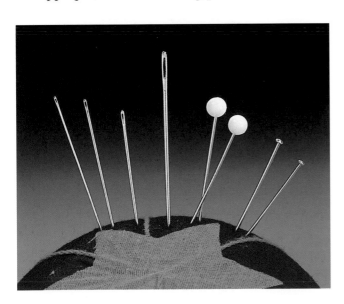

Left to right: Sharp needles, Between needle, Darning needle, ball-head pins, and dressmaking pins

Left to right: template plastic, manila folder, pencil, marker, sandpaper, ruler, and graph paper

Appliqué Needs

Spray starch. For hand appliqué, we use spray starch to make neat, turned-under seam allowances. We spray the starch into a glass jar, apply it to the fabric with a brush, and then twist a lid onto the jar to store any leftover starch.

Paintbrush. Use an inexpensive craft paintbrush to apply the starch.

Fusible web. For machine appliqué, use fusible web to adhere the appliqué patch onto the background fabric before stitching it in place. Purchase the kind with paper backing.

Nonstick baking parchment. Use baking parchment or a Teflon sheet to protect your iron and ironing surface when working with fusible web.

Stabilizer or paper. Use fabric stabilizer or lightweight paper to keep the stitching from puckering during machine appliqué.

Left to right: paintbrush, baking parchment, fusible web, stabilizer, and spray starch and jar

Equipment for Layering and Basting

Masking tape. This is used to attach a quilt backing onto a smooth surface so that it will remain flat during the basting process.

Bulldog or binder clips. Binder clips can be used to attach backing fabric onto a table for basting.

Safety pins. These are used to hold the layers of a quilt together for machine quilting. Depending on the size of your quilt, you may need several hundred pins. Choose rustproof safety pins 1" or 1½" [2.5 cm or 3.5 cm] long.

Bulldog clips, safety pins, and masking tape

Tools for Quilting

Tracing paper. This is used to trace quilting designs.

Chalk marker. A small-wheeled gadget that dispenses powdered chalk, this is used to mark lines for hand and machine quilting.

Soap slivers. Thin, dried-out remnants of soap are an alternative to a chalk marker.

Freezer paper. When ironed, freezer paper adheres to fabric. It can be used for shapes that are pressed to the fabric and quilted around.

Quilting stencils. These are sheets of plastic with designs cut into them. They are used to mark repeated designs.

Quilting hoop. A hoop is used to hold the quilt layers together for hand quilting. Choose a size that suits the length of your arm; your fingers holding the needle must be able to reach the center of the hoop with your elbows bent. A hoop between 14" and 18" [35 cm and 45 cm] in diameter is the usual size.

Thimbles and finger protectors. Thimbles protect your fingers while hand quilting. There are many possibilities here, and the choice is a personal one. A thimble that fits well will not squeeze your finger, nor will it drop off when you hold your finger upside down. The thimble for the sewing hand should fit your middle finger, to protect it as you push the needle through the quilt layers. The index finger on the other hand also needs protection because it guides the needle back up through the quilt layers. The index finger needs either a thimble without a ridge at its top or some other form of protection, such as an adhesive leather patch, an adhesive metal tip, a plastic protector, or a leather thimble with a metal tip.

Cotton gloves with rubber fingertips or latex gloves. These may be used for free-motion machine quilting to help improve your grip on the quilt layers.

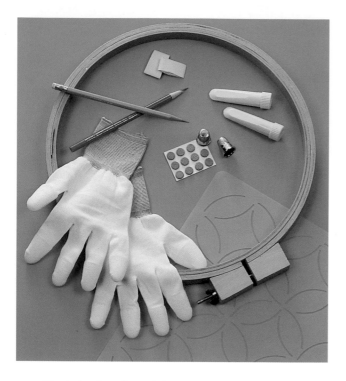

Clockwise from lower left: cotton gloves with rubber fingertips, pencils, tailor's chalk, chalk markers, thimbles, finger protectors, quilting hoop, and stencil

Design Area

Ideally, it is good to be able to put your patchwork onto a design wall so that you can stand back and see how your design and colors are working. A pin board is perfect for this, but as a good substitute you can tape cotton flannel around a sheet of foam core. Pinning a piece of batting onto curtains also makes a quick and easy design wall, or you can lay out your patchwork on a large floor space or a bed (a time-honored method). Create further distance by looking at your work through a camera, through the wrong end of binoculars, or through a door peephole (a fairly inexpensive item available at hardware stores).

Viewing patchwork on a design wall

Fabric and Supplies

Cotton is generally the fabric of choice for quiltmaking. A medium-weight cotton fabric is preferred because it offers the perfect combination of being easy to work with while you are making the quilt, and good to live with when the quilt is finished.

Cotton washes well, it can be cut cleanly, it is easy to sew, and it responds crisply to pressing. It is also a comfortable natural fiber to have next to the body. Today marvelous cotton fabrics are available in every possible hue and style of print, making quilt shops a visual feast of colors and designs.

Understanding Fabrics

The cotton fabric used in quilts is made by weaving (in contrast to fabric made by knitting, as in T-shirts, for example), and the threads are woven at right angles to each other. The direction of the threads is called the **straight grain** of the fabric. The fabric in these directions will have little or no stretch. The direction going diagonally across the threads at a 45° angle is called the **bias**, and this direction has maximum stretch.

It is important to understand the straight grain and bias because they will affect every seam that you sew. Pieces of fabric cut on the straight grain will hardly stretch while you are cutting, sewing, and pressing, while pieces cut on the bias will tend to stretch easily. While this bias stretch can cause difficulties if not handled carefully, it also can be used deliberately in appliqué to make strips that curve.

The side edges of woven fabric are called **selvages**. These edges are woven a bit more tightly than the rest of the fabric. Sometimes they are fringed, and they might not be colored or printed. These edges are cut off and not used in quilt-making.

Selvage edges

The width of woven cotton fabric is usually about 42" [106 cm]. With the selvages taken off, there is approximately 40" [100 cm] of usable fabric across the width.

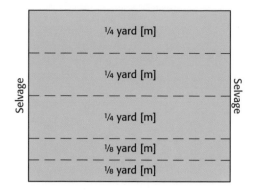

Fabrics are sold in yards [meters] or parts thereof. Half and quarter yards are respectively 18" and 9" long [half and quarter meters are 50 cm and 25 cm long]. A quarter of a yard is 9" x 40" [a quarter of a meter is 25 cm x 100 cm]; it is a long narrow rectangle of fabric. Quilters have realized that a more useful shape for patchwork is wider than this, so a yard or meter is frequently divided into quarters by first cutting the fabric across the width into half-yard [half-meter] segments, and then cutting these segments lengthwise down the center to make what quilters call a **fat quarter**. A fat quarter usually measures 18" x 21" [50 cm x 53 cm]. A **fat eighth** is made by cutting a fat quarter in half so that it measures 9" x 21" [25 cm x 53 cm].

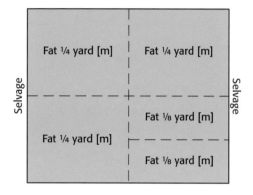

FABRIC GRAIN EXERCISE

Get a first-hand feel for fabric grain with this little stretch test.
You will need: a piece of woven cotton fabric and a magnifying glass (optional).

1. Pick up the piece of fabric and take a close look at it, either with the naked eye or using the magnifying glass. Notice how the threads on the fabric go under and over each other at right angles. The direction of the threads determines the straight grain of the fabric.

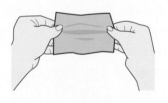

2. With your hands about 4" [10 cm] apart, pinch a bit of the fabric in each hand along the straight grain and pull. Then try pinching and pulling the fabric at a right angle to your first pull, and you should notice a slight difference—either more or less—in the amount of stretch. In one direction, the fabric stretches hardly at all. (This is the warp, or length of the fabric.) In the perpendicular direction, the amount of stretch is just a bit greater, although still small. (This is the weft, or crosswise grain of the fabric.) Both these directions are on the straight grain of the fabric.

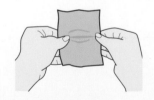

3. Now pinch two opposite corners of the fabric and pull; you will find the fabric stretches a lot more than on your previous tugs. This is the bias.

Most cotton quiltmaking fabrics are printed with colors and patterns on one side of the fabric, so the side with the definite print or color is called the right side of the fabric and the other side is the wrong side.

Choosing Fabrics

To successfully choose a group of fabrics for a quilt, you need to understand three important characteristics of fabrics—color, value, and print style.

Understanding Color

We all know the colors—yellow, orange, red, purple, blue, green, black, and white—and the myriad shades created by mixing these colors together in different proportions. Color is a vital ingredient in making your fabric choices, as color is usually the characteristic that most appeals to us in a finished quilt. There is a glorious range of colored fabrics available for quilters. Some colors or color combinations will appeal to you more than others. Choose colors to suit your own taste.

When you look at a color, examine its qualities by describing it to yourself. Take a red print, for example. Some reds have a bluish tinge, making them cherry red or even magenta. Other reds have more of an orange cast, like tomato red. The fabric may be dark red because it is tinged with black, or lighter red if it is tinged with white. Look at the following photograph to see just how different red prints can be. Understanding subtle

A variety of red prints

differences in color can make you more aware of exactly what color you are looking at. In turn, this will help you choose other colors to go with the fabric you've selected.

Fabric comes in a glorious range of colors.

The bright pink print adds a
color accent to this group of fabrics.

To determine what color a fabric really is, look at your fabrics from a distance to see how they "read." You might find, for example, that viewed close up your fabric has an interesting print of red and green. Seen from a distance, however, it reads as a brown. Generally, how a color reads at a distance will be how the color will work in your quilt.

Often quilts benefit from a small amount of a bright color, which is called an **accent color**. Because only a little of the fabric is used, the color can be more intense than other colors you have chosen. In the example at left, cover and then uncover the bright pink fabric with your finger. Without the bright pink accent, the combination is less exciting.

COLOR EXERCISE

The best way to learn about color is simply to become more consciously aware of the colors that surround you. It is easy to take color for granted, but if you stop and really look at the colors in your life—in a flower, a rock, a leaf, a painting, a sunset, a photograph, in advertisements—you will learn a lot.

You will need: a few full-color magazines.

1. Find a magazine picture that visually appeals to you. Analyze exactly what colors are in it. Don't just say "blue," but analyze what kind of blue, such as gray-blue, green-blue, and so on. Notice any accent colors.

2. Find a picture that appears bright and vibrant. Analyze what colors are used.

3. Find a picture that appears calm and tranquil. Analyze what colors are used.

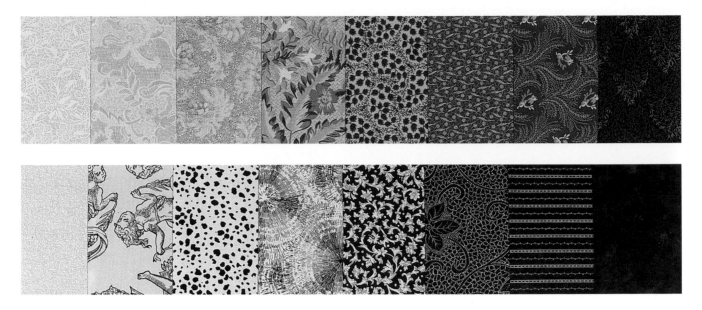

Fabrics arranged in value scales from light to dark

Value

Value, or tonal value, means how light or dark a fabric is. All fabrics can be arranged in a value scale, which means they can be arranged from lightest to darkest. Pure black and pure white are obviously the darkest and lightest colors, and everything else fits in between. Regardless of color and print style, each fabric can be put somewhere on a value scale.

There are several ways to determine the values in a group of fabrics. The easiest way is to squint so that you cut out most of the light. When you do so, the value will stand out more than the color, helping you to see if one fabric is lighter or darker than another. Looking at fabrics from a distance also helps, so group the fabrics together and walk away; then look at them again. Reading fabrics from a distance is a very useful exercise, because it helps you see how the fabrics will work together as a group within the quilt. You can also look at the fabrics through a camera lens or the wrong end of binoculars. This has the effect of making the fabrics look farther away. A reducing glass also works, or a door peephole.

You may intuitively think that color is the most important factor in quiltmaking, but it is the variation in value that makes the patchwork pattern appear. As an example, look at the following blocks. The block on the left uses three different fabrics, but the values are much the same, so the pattern does not show up. The block on the right also contains only three fabrics, and the center square is the same fabric as in the first block, but there is more contrast in value, which lets you see the star pattern more clearly.

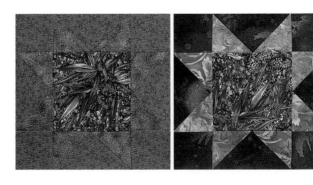

The block on the left has less contrast in values.
The block on the right has higher contrast in values,
showing the patchwork design.

It is important to understand that value is relative in any group of fabrics. The same fabric can be light in one context, a medium value in another group, and dark in a third set of fabrics. The value of a fabric is determined by its neighbors.

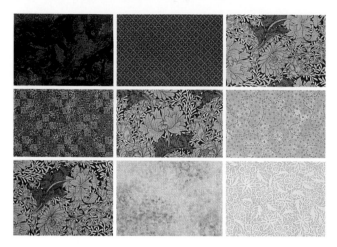

The same fabric (the floral print) can be light, medium, or dark, depending on its context.

You can make the relativity of value work for you in your quilts. You may want to make a bold statement by choosing a big difference in value in your fabrics, or you may want to create a more subtle effect by choosing more similarity in values. But either way, there must be some difference between the values of the fabrics so that the patchwork design is readable.

It's difficult to assign value to some fabrics, especially those that mix extreme darks and lights fairly equally, such as a print with equal amounts of black and white. These fabrics have a striking but jumpy look to them. They can make great accents in a quilt, but may be too overwhelming in large quantities.

Fabrics mixing equal amounts of light and dark

VALUE EXERCISE

Practice working with value using scraps cut from magazine pages before cutting into your fabrics.

You will need: used full-color magazines and a pair of scissors.

1. Choose a color and then search through some magazines looking for various shades of that color. Cut out small strips of about 10 to 12 different shades of the color ranging from light to dark. It is easiest to use solid areas of color. Cut pieces about 3/8" x 1" [1 cm x 3 cm] each, but they can vary. Arrange the strips from light to dark to make a tonal scale.

2. Cut 10 to 12 strips of other colors. Arrange the strips from light to dark as you did for the first color.

3. Mix the colors and combine the two ranges into one long strip.

4. Pick a strip from the middle of the range. Combine it with two other lighter strips so that you have three values, with the mid-value strip now being the darkest.

5. Combine the mid-value strip with two other darker strips to make the strip the lightest value in the group.

Print Style

Print style refers to the kind of pattern or design that is printed on the fabric. You'll find a huge range of styles available, with large- and small-scale prints, sparse and close motifs, geometric patterns, floral designs, stripes, polka dots, abstracts, checks, and plaids. Avoid using print styles that are all of the same size or scale. Patchwork that contains only small-scale prints may look boring, while all large-scale prints may be overwhelming. Rather, combine a variety of prints to make your quilt visually interesting.

It is preferable to mix print scales (bottom) rather than have all small-scale prints (top left) or all large-scale prints (top right).

Quilters give special names to some styles of fabrics.

- **Solids.** These fabrics are just one color with no printed pattern or variation within the color.
- **Tone-on-tone prints.** These are subtle prints made of different values of one color.
- **Feature fabrics.** These fabrics have prominent pictorial motifs or special subject matter; they are also called theme fabrics. This type of print is often the dominant fabric in a quilt.
- **Hand-dyed prints.** Similar to true hand-dyed fabrics, these commercial prints have uneven background color.

- **Batiks.** These fabrics are dyed, stamped with a pattern, and overdyed.

Left to right: solids, tone-on-tone prints, feature fabrics, hand-dyed prints, and batiks

- **Background fabrics.** As the name suggests, background fabrics are the backdrop against which the other fabrics in the quilt or block are placed. A background fabric can be any color, value, or print style, as long as the quilt's patchwork design stands out and does not disappear into it.

Background choices range from light to dark, calm to busy.

- **Directional fabrics.** These have a design that goes in only one direction. Stripes are the most obvious example, but many other designs can have directional motifs. Some are quite subtle, as only close inspection reveals that they are in fact directional. If you want to have stripes or a directional fabric go in a particular direction in your block or quilt, you must consciously cut the pieces to achieve this. It may take some planning to use directional fabrics, but it's worth it for the zing they can add to a design.

Directional fabrics

Selecting Fabrics for Your Quilt

So how do you choose a group of fabrics for a quilt? A good way to begin is to find a fabric you really like and then choose other fabrics to go with it. The fabric can be a feature fabric or any fabric that particularly appeals to you. Look at the color or colors in your chosen fabric and use these to suggest other fabrics. The colors don't have to match exactly. You can choose lighter or darker versions of colors in your main fabric or look for fabrics that you like together in a group. Include a background fabric in your mix and see if an accent fabric will give the whole group some pizzazz.

Look at the fabric groupings above. Each group includes a background fabric at the top, a feature fabric at the bottom, and a range of values and print styles. Notice how the colors in each group are selected from the feature fabric.

When selecting fabric for the back of your quilt, choose cotton fabrics the same weight as the fabrics in the quilt top. Avoid using sheets or sheeting, as they may not be 100% cotton and may have a tighter weave than standard quilting cotton, which makes quilting difficult. Most quilters look for bargain fabrics for their quilt backs, taking advantage of sales or closeout fabrics at reduced prices. Whatever you choose, try to coordinate the back with the front of the quilt, so that the back gives pleasure, too.

CHOOSING QUILT FABRICS

No matter how you go about choosing your fabrics, try to follow these four principles:

- Always try fabrics together in a group. Place the pieces or bolts of fabric next to each other, arranging them roughly in proportion to how you think you might use them. For example, show more of a print you might use a lot of as a background, less of one that is going to be an accent. Try different fabrics in the group by putting in and taking out one fabric at a time. Don't forget to look at them from a distance.

- Make sure that the group includes a range of values. You need some light-dark contrast to carry the patchwork design.

- Include a variety of print styles. Avoid using only one kind of print in a quilt. For example, if you have already chosen a large-scale print, select a smaller-scale print to go with it, contrast a floral with a geometric, and so on.

- Please yourself. Make sure you're happy with your final selection. After all, it's your quilt!

Washing Fabrics

We recommend that you prewash all fabrics before using them. As the old adage says, it is better to be safe than sorry. The color in some fabrics does run, and fabrics can also shrink slightly in the wash. Group your fabrics in colors as you would laundry, washing light colors together, dark colors together, and washing separately any fabric you are suspicious of (some hand-dyed fabrics and red prints in particular). Wash fabrics on a gentle cycle with a little mild detergent, or soak them in a bucket of hot water. Air dry if possible, or remove fabrics from the dryer before they are fully dry so that creases are not set in.

It is not necessary to iron fabrics after they have been washed and dried. Just fold them and put them away. However, always iron your fabrics before you begin to cut. The ironing makes them crisp and smooth as well as wrinkle- and crease-free. Pressing fabrics before cutting makes your cutting more accurate.

Calculating Fabric Quantities

At first, calculating how much fabric you will need won't be a problem, as we suggest you follow published instructions for your first few quilts, such as those in this book. But it is valuable to know how to figure out how much fabric you'll need, so we suggest that you come back to this section when you need it.

Taking one fabric at a time, determine what shapes will be cut from each fabric. Then, for each shape, work out how many will be needed for the whole quilt. Next, work out how many shapes fit in a strip of fabric across the 40" [100 cm] width.

A calculator is invaluable for this task! Divide the total number of shapes needed by the number you can cut from one strip to determine how many strips are required. Then, multiply the number of strips by the length of the shape to give a subtotal of how much fabric is required for that shape. Repeat this for all the shapes to be cut from that fabric. Add up all the subtotals to make the final total for the fabric. Round up to the nearest quarter yard [10 cm] to make up for the fabric that will be lost in the washing process and in cutting the first straight edge.

Repeat this process for each fabric. To avoid joins or to take advantage of a directional print, borders often need to be cut lengthwise. When that's the case, work out border requirements first, and then use the remaining fabric as required.

It may help to sketch your calculations onto a piece of paper, drawing the shapes into as many rows as are required to achieve the correct number, and noting the size.

Batting

Batting (or wadding) is a thin padding made from cotton, polyester, wool, or a blend of these. There are a great variety of battings, each with its own characteristics. To select the batting that best suits your plans, read labels and ask your quilt shop for information. Both cotton and wool battings breathe well and are natural products, although they are sometimes enhanced with polyester to decrease the required density of quilting. Some cotton battings are suitable for both hand and machine quilting, while others are harder to needle by hand. Polyester batting is light and easily washed. It is also easy to hand quilt, but it can slip more easily during free-motion quilting. Some battings have a higher **loft** than others, which means they puff up more between lines of quilting. Other battings have a lower loft and give a flatter look. Dark-colored batting is recommended for black and dark-colored quilts to avoid noticeable

Clockwise from upper left: wool, dark polyester, light polyester, and cotton batting

bearding. (**Bearding** refers to batting fibers coming through the top of the quilt. Light fibers coming through a dark quilt top can be conspicuous.) Batting is sold in wide lengths from a roll, as well as in packages precut to various bed sizes. Purchase batting 4" [10 cm] larger (in length and width) than the size of your quilt top.

Threads

For piecing, appliqué, and machine quilting, use good-quality threads suitable for general-purpose sewing. Some people prefer to use pure cotton threads to be consistent with the cotton fabrics, but this is personal preference, as there are high-quality polyester and cotton-covered polyester threads, too. Avoid bargain threads; some have a fluffy surface and others may melt when ironed.

For piecing, choose a thread color that blends with the fabrics you are sewing: light thread for light-colored fabrics, dark thread for dark-colored fabrics, or a medium-value color, such as light brown or gray, when you are combining dark and light colors. For appliqué, choose a color that matches each fabric piece to be appliquéd, not the background fabric.

For hand quilting, it is essential to use a quilting thread that has been specially manufactured to be strong for hand quilting. Do not use hand-quilting thread in your sewing machine.

For machine appliqué using the fusible method, use machine-embroidery thread (a more lightly twisted thread) on the top of the machine and a bobbin fill or fine cotton in the bobbin.

Left to right: threads for piecing and appliqué, hand quilting, and machine appliqué

Understanding the Patch System

Thousands of wonderful traditional patchwork blocks exist, designs just waiting for you. Two keys will unlock the secrets of most traditional quilt blocks for you. The first key is knowing the three most common shapes found in quilt blocks. The second key is understanding the **patch system**, or the way blocks can be divided into grids. This knowledge will put the world of quiltmaking at your fingertips.

Three Basic Shapes

There are three basic shapes used in most traditional pieced quilt blocks.

Squares and rectangles. Both squares and rectangles have four sides, with a right angle (90° angle) in each corner. Squares have four sides of equal length, while rectangles have two shorter and two longer sides.

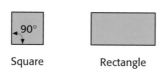

Square   Rectangle

Half-square triangles. These are triangles made by cutting a square in half diagonally. Half-square triangles have a right angle in one corner. The long side is cut on the bias.

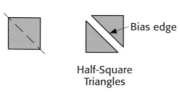

Half-Square
Triangles

Quarter-square triangles. These are triangles made by cutting a square into quarters, dividing it across both diagonals. Quarter-square triangles also have a right angle in one corner. The two short sides are cut on the bias.

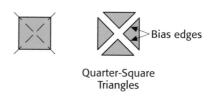

Quarter-Square
Triangles

While half-square and quarter-square triangles look alike at first glance, they are not interchangeable within a patchwork design. They both have right angles and two equal-length sides, but they are cut differently on the fabric grain, which makes all the difference in how they are used in a block. Generally, pieces at the perimeter of a block should be on the straight grain of fabric so that the edges of the block won't stretch out of shape.

Project directions generally specify when you need to cut one type of triangle or the other.

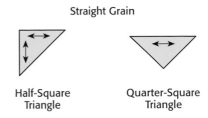

Straight Grain

Half-Square Triangle   Quarter-Square Triangle

Of course, squares and rectangles, half-square triangles, and quarter-square triangles are not the only possible shapes for quiltmaking. Just about any geometric shape you can imagine is used for patchwork quilt blocks, including diamonds, hexagons, all kinds of triangles, and even curved shapes. These other shapes are beyond the scope of this book, however. We'll introduce you to the most important and commonly used shapes to give you a solid basis on which to build later.

The Patch System

Patchwork blocks are the design units used to make a quilt. Generally (although not always), patchwork blocks are square. The square shape is divided into a grid of smaller squares, or patches. Understanding the patch system is the second key to patchwork.

A square block can be divided in several different ways—by two, three, four, five, or seven. Over time, quiltmakers have grouped blocks using the same divisions and given them names. The system is quite logical and simple, although the names aren't quite as logical. The nine-patch is named for the number of squares in the grid, even though the number of divisions is three. On the other hand, the five-patch and seven-patch blocks are named by the number of divisions. A four-patch can refer to either the number of squares in the grid or the

number of divisions. As soon as you understand the grid that determines the patch system, you will quickly become familiar with the names.

Four-patch. A block that can be divided by either two or four is called a four-patch.

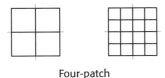

Four-patch

Nine-patch. A block that is divided by three is called a nine-patch.

Nine-patch

Five-patch. A block that is divided by five is called a five-patch.

Five-patch

Seven-patch. A block that can be divided by seven is called a seven-patch.

Seven-patch

Note that a block is classified by its major divisions, although blocks can be further divided within the major divisions. For you, the main thing is to be able to look at a block and work out what the major divisions are. Simply ask yourself, will the block divide by two or four? By three, five, or seven?

Putting Shapes and Patches Together

Patchwork blocks are created by putting shapes into the grid of patches. The possibilities are exciting and endless! Once the squares, rectangles, half-square triangles, and quarter-square triangles are inserted into the grid, then parts of the design can be shaded in different values of dark and light to make the patchwork block.

Adding Half-Square Triangles to
a Four-Patch Grid

Adding Quarter-Square Triangles
to a Nine-Patch Grid

Many quilt blocks are old designs from tiling patterns that can be found in floors from ancient times. As patchwork became popular, designs were passed on from quiltmaker to quiltmaker. Old designs were altered and new designs emerged in a true folk tradition. Quiltmakers gave names to the block designs, the most obvious being Four Patch and Nine Patch. These names directly reflect the grids upon which the blocks are based, but blocks were also given names to reflect items in daily life, such as places, everyday objects, famous people, birds, political figures, and religious beliefs.

Quilt blocks often acquired different names in different places. For example, the Bear's Paw block has also been called Duck's Foot and Hand of Friendship. There are many books available that explain name derivations, but in this book we refer to blocks by the names commonly used today.

Filling in the grid with patchwork shapes is just the beginning. You can vary block designs in many ways, such as reversing the values or introducing mid-values in addition to lights and darks.

Drawing a Block

By understanding the patch or grid system, you will always be able to draw a block quickly and easily. Once you know how many patches a block has, you can draw a square in a size that is divisible by that number of patches. Then you can simply draw the shapes into the patches and shade them to make the patchwork block. To make your block perfectly square, draw it on graph paper.

Draw grid.   Draw shapes.

Shade to make block.

You can approach determining a block's size in one of two ways. First, you can determine how big you want your individual patches to be and then multiply this size by the number of patches in your grid. For example, for a five-patch block with 2" [5 cm] patches, the size of the block will be 5 x 2", or 10" [5 x 5 cm, or 25 cm]. Second, you can start with how big you want your finished block to be, and work backward. If you know you want a 12" [30 cm] finished block, and you plan to make a nine-patch block, divide the block size by 3 to determine that each patch needs to be 4" [10 cm].

It is generally easiest to work from the patch size to the block size, as that way you can deal with whole numbers. Dividing 10" [25 cm] by 3 just doesn't work neatly. However, 10" works fine for a five-patch block.

Other Patchwork Designs

Not all patchwork designs fit neatly into a block or grid category. Following are a few perennial favorites among quiltmakers.

One-patch designs are made by repeating a single shape, such as a square, rectangle, triangle, hexagon, or diamond.

Trip Around the World

Roman Stripe

Brickwall

Log Cabin blocks are made from a central square surrounded by successive strips or "logs." Log Cabin blocks are traditionally made with half the block composed of light strips and the other half of dark strips, which enables you to create all sorts of interesting designs when setting the blocks together in a quilt (see page 95).

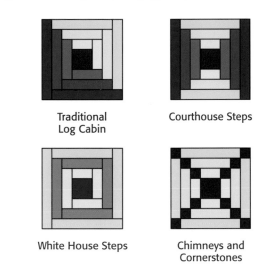

Traditional Log Cabin

Courthouse Steps

White House Steps

Chimneys and Cornerstones

Flying Geese are rows of quarter-square triangles flanked by half-square triangles.

Of course, there are many more possibilities of block designs based on other shapes, but for this book we'll focus on the basic types presented here.

Library of Classic Blocks

Following is a small library of best-loved block designs.

Short lines outside the blocks indicate the grid divisions.

Four-patch blocks

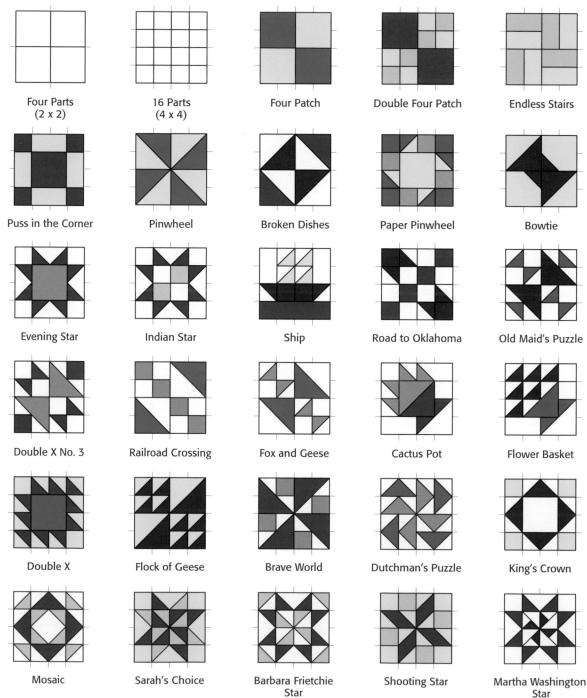

Four Parts (2 x 2)	16 Parts (4 x 4)	Four Patch	Double Four Patch	Endless Stairs
Puss in the Corner	Pinwheel	Broken Dishes	Paper Pinwheel	Bowtie
Evening Star	Indian Star	Ship	Road to Oklahoma	Old Maid's Puzzle
Double X No. 3	Railroad Crossing	Fox and Geese	Cactus Pot	Flower Basket
Double X	Flock of Geese	Brave World	Dutchman's Puzzle	King's Crown
Mosaic	Sarah's Choice	Barbara Frietchie Star	Shooting Star	Martha Washington Star

Four-patch blocks (continued)

Whirligig

Pinwheel II

Seesaw

Next Door Neighbor

Windmill Square

Yankee Puzzle

Snail's Trail

Devil's Claws

Kansas Troubles

State House

Nine-patch blocks

Nine Parts
(3 x 3)

36 Parts
(6 x 6)

Nine Patch

Snowball

Shoo Fly

Friendship Star

Split Nine Patch

Spools

Churn Dash

Double X

Birds in the Air

North Wind

Ribbon Quilt

Milky Way

Contrary Wife

Sailboat

Jacob's Ladder

Steps to the Alter

Prairie Queen

Album

Ohio Star

Swamp Angel

Card Trick

Aunt Dinah

Memory

Nine-patch blocks (continued)

Weathervane

Aunt Sukey's Choice

Eddystone Light

Corn and Beans

Cut Glass Dish

Rosebud

Capital T

Five-patch blocks

25 Parts
(5 x 5)

Country Lanes

Sister's Choice

Double Wrench

Duck and Ducklings

Lady of the Lake

Delectable Mountains

Fruit Basket

Spinning Tops

Old Fashioned
Wedding Ring

Jack in the Box

Joseph's Coat

Seven-patch blocks

49 Parts
(7 x 7)

Bear's Paw

Lincoln's Platform

Dove in the
Window

Buffalo Ridge

Autumn Tints

Ribbon Block

Prickly Pear

Piecing

Piecing is the technique of joining patches of

fabric side by side to make a design.

Pieces of fabric are joined with lines of stitching called seams. The pieces are cut out a little larger all around than the size desired, and then they are sewn together, leaving a small amount of fabric beyond the stitching to make sure the seam does not unravel. The narrow strip of fabric between the stitching and the cut edge is called the **seam allowance**. Seam allowances are always measured at right angles—that is, perpendicular— to the seam line.

 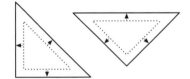

The **cut size** of a patch is its size including the seam allowance. The standard seam allowance used in quiltmaking is ¼" [7.5 mm]. The **finished size** of a patch is its size without the seam allowance. It is the size of a patch or block that you see on the front of the finished quilt. Understanding finished size is critical for quiltmaking because all cutting measurements for machine piecing are based on adding the seam allowances to the finished size of each patch. If you both cut and sew

the seam allowances accurately, all of the pieces will fit together beautifully.

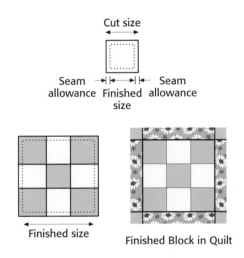

Cut size

Seam allowance — Finished size — Seam allowance

Finished size

Finished Block in Quilt

Quilts are easier and more enjoyable to make when the patches are cut accurately so that they will fit together nicely. Accuracy counts in all phases of quiltmaking, from cutting to sewing to pressing. Taking the time to develop accurate habits is really worth the effort in the long run.

Rotary Cutting

The rotary cutter is your magic wand in the wonderful world of modern quiltmaking. This tool has revolutionized cutting, making the process quicker, easier, and above all, more accurate.

Rotary-Cutting Rulers

Rulers made specifically for rotary cutting are made of clear acrylic so that they are thick, durable, and you can see the fabric through them. They have grids printed on them so that they measure length and width at the same time. Once the ruler is placed accurately on your fabric, the rotary cutter is rolled along the edge of the ruler to cut the fabric.

The Cutting Action

The rotary cutter is held in your **dominant hand**, the right hand for right-handed people and the left hand for left-handed people. Your other hand will hold the ruler in place. If you're right-handed, always cut on the right side of the ruler; if you're left-handed, always cut on the left side. To avoid confusing you by stating left or right hand in the instructions, we simply call the hand holding the cutter the "cutting hand" and the hand holding the ruler the "ruler hand."

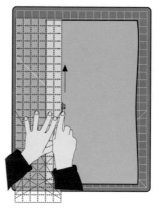 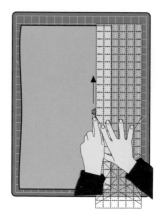

Right-Handed   Left-Handed

ESSENTIAL ROTARY-CUTTER SAFETY

Knowing how to use a rotary cutter safely is a must for every quilter. Rotary cutters are very sharp, and the blade will cut skin as easily as fabric. It is vitally important that you follow these rules:

- Keep the blade guard closed whenever you are not actually cutting fabric. Never lay down an open cutter. Make it a habit to close the cutter every time. Some cutters have a safety cover that is always in place except when the cutter is actually cutting, so you may want to try one of these models.

- Keep your fingers on top of the ruler, completely away from the edge where the cutter will cut.

- Always cut away from yourself. The cutting action involves pushing forward from your body.

- Stand up for cutting. It will reduce the pressure and stretch on your shoulders, and you'll have better control over the pressure you can use on the cutter. Find the right cutting height for you. For many people, it is the height of a kitchen counter.

- Rotary cutting requires using pressure from both your hands as well as bending over to line up the ruler and push the cutter. These motions will be repeated many times, so it is important to take breaks frequently and to arch your back gently backward from time to time, to stretch your muscles into an opposite curve to your cutting position.

- Keep the cutter totally out of reach of young children.

We suggest you refer to this section closely as you begin trying the rotary-cutting action. Make several cuts to gain the feel of cutting smoothly. You'll need a pressed piece of fabric, a rotary cutter, a cutting mat, and a long ruler.

1. Position your cutting mat on the table so that the short edge of the mat is closest to you. This will give you the longest possible length to cut on as you roll the rotary cutter away from yourself.

2. Hold the ruler in place on the fabric by spreading out your fingers and thumb and applying pressure on the ruler with your fingertips, not the palm of your hand. Be sure to keep your fingers away from the cutting edge!

3. Hold the cutter firmly but comfortably in your cutting hand. As cutters vary in shape, the grip may vary a little from one brand to another. If possible, put your index finger on top of the grip to help you guide the cutter and keep your wrist from turning as you cut. If your cutter has a manual guard, flick the guard away from the blade just before you begin to cut.

4. Hold the cutter against the edge of the ruler so the blade is perpendicular to the ruler and cutting mat. Don't angle the cutter. The cutter must run smoothly exactly along the edge of the ruler.

5. Pushing the cutter away from your body, cut smoothly along the length of the ruler. Maintain an even pressure on both the ruler and the cutter as you cut all the way across the fabric. If you relax the pressure, you may find that some of the fabric is not cut and will need to be recut, which you want to avoid.

6. For a long cut, you may have to "walk" your hand along the ruler to maintain firm pressure at the area you are cutting. Do this very carefully so that your ruler does not move at all. Stop cutting, but keep the cutter in place beside the ruler; then move your ruler hand smoothly along by scooting your thumb up close to your fingers. Then move your fingers farther along the ruler. This way, your hand never entirely leaves the ruler, so you have less risk of it shifting out of place.

7. After each cut, close the safety guard. Never put down an open cutter.

CHANGING BLADES

Like any other cutting implement, a rotary-cutting blade will eventually become dull. If you notice that it takes a little more pressure to make clean cuts, or if your blade seems to be skipping threads as you cut, then it's time for a new blade.

To replace the cutter blade, dismantle the cutting head, carefully laying out the pieces in the order and orientation that you remove them. This way you will know exactly how to put the cutter back together again. To safely dispose of the old blade, put it in the packaging from the new blade when you discard it.

Preparing Fabric for Cutting

1. For accurate cutting, it is important to press the fabric first. Even previously ironed fabrics will have developed creases from being folded in storage.

2. Small pieces of fabric, such as fat quarters or scraps, can be laid directly on the cutting mat, but place them so that the fabric grain lines up with the grid lines on the cutting mat.

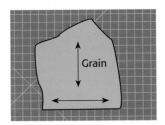

3. Most cuts are made across the width of the fabric. Fold the fabric in half lengthwise to fit on your cutting mat. While it is a natural instinct to fold fabric from the corners, you'll achieve a more accurate fold by holding the fabric at the center and adjusting the selvage edges until they are approximately aligned. Fabric isn't necessarily cut accurately at the shop, so don't be alarmed if the two cut or raw ends look crooked. That's quite common.

4. Lay the fabric on the cutting board with the folded edge closest to you, and you're ready to begin cutting.

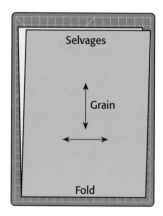

Making the First Cut

It is essential to first cut a straight edge on the fabric, as all the other cuts are measured against this edge. Cut this straight edge on the grain of the fabric so that some edges of your patches will be on the straight grain.

If you're working with a small piece of fabric such as a fat quarter, place the fabric so that the edge you are going to cut is on the side of your cutting hand and the bulk of the fabric is on the side of your ruler hand. Place the ruler so that it aligns parallel with the selvage. If your fabric is a scrap and doesn't have a selvage, align the ruler as closely as possible to the grain line, and cut. Turn

the fabric around so that the straight edge is on the side of your ruler hand, ready for the next cut.

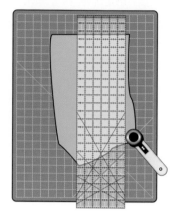

Straighten edge.

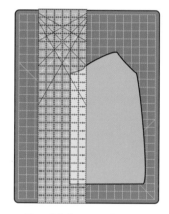

Turn fabric around to cut.

If you're working with a large piece of fabric that needs to be folded, the first straight cut must be made at an exact right angle to the fold in the fabric. To achieve this, the fold must be aligned with either the bottom edge of the ruler or a line parallel to the bottom edge. If you do not cut at a right angle, the fabric will be a crooked V shape when it is unfolded.

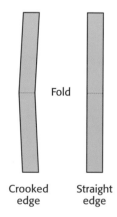

Crooked edge   Straight edge

Another concern with folded fabric is keeping the layers exactly in place. Moving the fabric may shift the layers, so that the straight cut edges will no longer be aligned. This will cause the next cut to be inaccurate for one or more of the layers.

To make an accurate and perpendicular first cut, you can use either of the following two methods.

Using Two Rulers

This method is extremely accurate, and since you don't need to move or turn the fabric, the layers stay exactly in place.

1. Place the fabric with the folded edge closest to you. Place the edge of the fabric you want to cut on the side of the ruler hand, with the bulk of the fabric on the side of the cutting hand.

2. Place the shorter of your rulers on the fabric near the edge you wish to cut, aligning the bottom edge of the ruler with the fold of the fabric.

3. Place the long ruler exactly alongside the first ruler and hold it firmly in place.

4. Remove the first ruler and cut down the length of the second ruler. The fabric is now ready for a second cut.

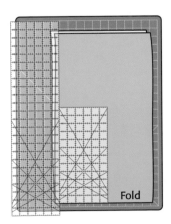
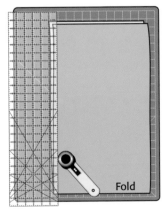

Align smaller ruler's edge on fold.   Cut along long ruler's edge.

Using One Long Ruler

This method is somewhat less desirable than the first method because either you or the fabric has to move after you make the first cut, which may disturb the layers.

1. Place the fabric so that the edge to be cut is on the side of your cutting hand and the bulk of the fabric is on the side of the ruler hand.

2. Line up the bottom of your long ruler with the fold of the fabric directly in front of you. Holding the ruler firmly in place, cut along the edge of the ruler.

3. To get ready for the next cut, carefully turn the mat, with the fabric on top, so that the straight edge is ready for the next cut. Be careful not to get the cut edges out of alignment. If you are cutting on a bench or table where you can work from either side, you can simply walk around to the other side and continue cutting instead of moving the mat and fabric.

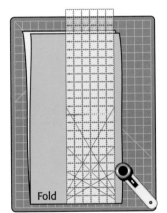
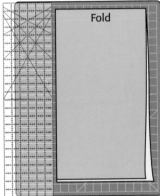

Cut to straighten edge.   Turn mat and fabric.

The 1/4" [7.5 mm] Seam Allowance

A 1/4" [7.5 mm] seam allowance is fundamental to rotary cutting and machine piecing. This means that the distance between the stitching (the finished size) and the cut edge must be exactly 1/4" [7.5 mm]. All cutting measurements for machine piecing are based on adding this seam allowance to the finished size of each patch. You must always both cut and sew the exact seam allowance, so that all the pieces will fit together beautifully.

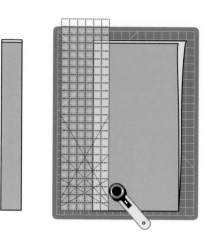

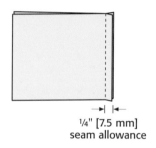

1/4" [7.5 mm]
seam allowance

Cutting Strips

Strips are the basis for cutting most other shapes; they can be crosscut to make rectangles and squares, and squares can be further crosscut to make triangles. Strips are cut in different widths according to the final size and shape that you need for your patchwork blocks.

To cut strips, align the clean-cut edge of the fabric with a line on the ruler that corresponds to the width of the strip desired. Make sure that the cut edge and the line on the ruler are exactly aligned along the whole length of fabric. Also check to make sure that the bottom of the ruler or one of the cross gridlines is aligned with the fold. This will ensure that your strips won't be V-shaped when opened up.

For example, if you want to cut a 2" [5 cm] strip, the ruler should be placed so that the 2" [5 cm] line is placed exactly on the straight edge of the fabric. The edge of the ruler is now 2" [5 cm] away from the straight edge of the fabric. By cutting along the edge of the ruler, you will cut a strip exactly 2" [5 cm] wide.

RESTRAIGHTENING THE EDGES

After cutting a couple strips of folded fabric, check that the straight edge is still perpendicular to the fold. Often it will not be, so you need to restraighten the cut edge. This will ensure that your strips continue to be straight as you work your way across the fabric.

To cut strips that are wider than your long ruler, use two rulers side by side. For instance, if you need strips that are 9" [24 cm] wide, place your shorter ruler so the 3" [8 cm] line is on the cut edge of the fabric and your 6" [16 cm]-wide long ruler is butted up against it. Then cut along the edge of the long ruler and you'll have a 9" [24 cm]-wide strip.

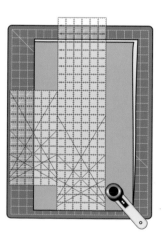

Crosscutting Shapes

Remember, each patch needs to have ¼" [7.5 mm]-wide seam allowances added to it. In project directions, cut sizes are given with the seam allowance already added. But when you're ready to make your own blocks, you'll need to know just how much to add in order to cut shapes that include the seam allowances. The amount varies according to the shape of the patch, and we call that amount the "magic number." In the next sections, we describe how to cut each shape from strips, and we give you the magic numbers so that you'll be able to cut squares, rectangles, or triangles of any size, each with its exact ¼" [7.5 mm] seam allowance all around.

Squares and Rectangles

The magic number for cutting squares and rectangles is ½" [1.5 cm] added to the finished size. This results in ¼" [7.5 mm] all around the finished size.

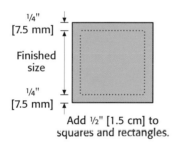

¼" [7.5 mm]

Finished size

¼" [7.5 mm]

Add ½" [1.5 cm] to squares and rectangles.

1. Cut a strip of fabric the required width, which is the finished width of your square or rectangle plus ½" [1.5 cm].

2. Square up the end (or ends, if the strip is folded) of the strip by placing the end to be cut on the side of your cutting hand. Place the ruler near the end of the strip so that a horizontal line on the ruler exactly aligns with the bottom cut edge of the strip. Make the cut.

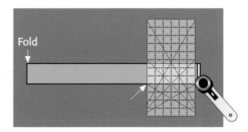

Place a line on the ruler on the edge of the strip.

3. Turn the strip around so that the straight-cut end is now on your ruler-hand side, keeping the edges exactly aligned. Measure and cut from the straight edge. For squares, measure the same distance as the strip width. For rectangles, measure the length needed. Further shapes can be cut against each succeeding cut edge.

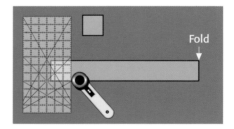

TIPS FOR SQUARES

- If you are crosscutting lots of shapes along a strip, check from time to time that you are cutting exactly at right angles. If you find that the end of your strip is a little crooked (which does happen), square up the end and continue crosscutting.

- Cutting time is halved if you cut strips that are folded or two strips that are laid exactly one on top of the other. If the strip is folded, be careful to keep the cut edges of the strip aligned when cutting. Do not try to cut more than two layers until you are more experienced, as more layers easily lead to inaccurate cutting.

- Cut individual squares and rectangles in two steps: Cut along one side and the top of the square, and then flip the shape around and cut the other two sides.

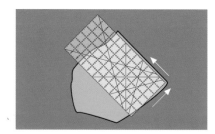

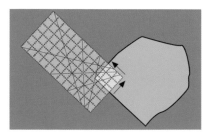

Half-Square Triangles

Half-square triangles are made when a square is cut in half diagonally to yield two triangles. The magic number is ⅞" [2.5 cm] added to the finished size of a square. Adding this amount will result in ¼" [7.5 mm] seam allowances on all sides of the two triangles.

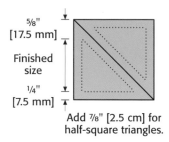

⅝" [17.5 mm]

Finished size

¼" [7.5 mm]

Add ⅞" [2.5 cm] for half-square triangles.

1. Cut a strip of fabric the required width (the finished size of the square plus ⅞" [2.5 cm]).

2. Square the end of the strip and crosscut the strip into squares.

3. Cut each square in half diagonally, cutting exactly from corner to corner.

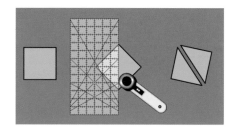

Quarter-Square Triangles

Quarter-square triangles are made when a square is cut diagonally in both directions to yield four triangles. The magic number is 1¼" [3.5 cm] added to the finished size of a square. Adding this amount will result in ¼" [7.5 mm] seam allowances on all sides of the four triangles.

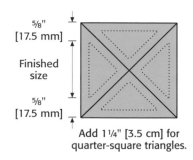

⅝" [17.5 mm]

Finished size

⅝" [17.5 mm]

Add 1¼" [3.5 cm] for quarter-square triangles.

1. Cut a strip of fabric the required width (the finished size of the square plus 1¼" [3.5 cm]).

2. Square the end of the strip and crosscut the strip into squares.

3. Cut each square in half diagonally, cutting exactly from corner to corner.

4. Carefully lift the ruler, leaving the two halves of the fabric square exactly in place. Realign the ruler across the opposite diagonal and cut from corner to corner.

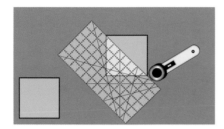

Cut one diagonal. Do not move pieces.

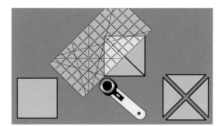

Cut opposite diagonal.

MAGIC NUMBERS

Remember these magic numbers for adding seam allowances to common shapes:

- To cut squares and rectangles, add ½" [1.5 cm] to the finished size of the square or rectangle

- To cut half-square triangles, add ⅞" [2.5 cm] to the finished size of the square.

- To cut quarter-square triangles, add 1¼" [3.5 cm] to the finished size of the square.

Cutting Lengthwise Strips

Some projects will require longer strips than those cut across the width of the fabric. Borders are often cut lengthwise down the fabric so that you don't need to piece strips together to fit the quilt. When a directional fabric is used for borders or long sashing, it may be necessary to cut along the length of the fabric so that the printed design shows up nicely on the finished quilt.

To cut lengthwise strips, fold the fabric across its width, aligning the selvage edges. Make as many parallel folds as needed to fit the fabric on the length of the mat (the fabric may extend off the mat sideways). Place a folded edge near you, orienting it horizontally. Use the two-ruler method (see page 39) to cut the first straight edge.

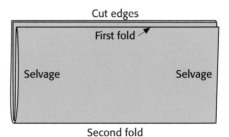

Cutting Bias Strips

Bias strips are sometimes required for appliqué and for quilt binding. Quilts with curved edges need bias binding, and if you're using a stripe or plaid, you may like the look of the design cut diagonally.

1. Lay the fabric in a single layer on the cutting mat, with a straight-grain edge directly in front of you.

2. Place your ruler on the fabric, matching the 45° line on the ruler with the straight edge of the fabric. The length of the ruler should now be at a 45° angle sloping away from your cutting hand and going toward your ruler hand, as shown.

3. Cut along the length of the ruler. The edge of the fabric will be on the bias. You can discard the triangle you cut off, or toss it in your scrap basket for another project.

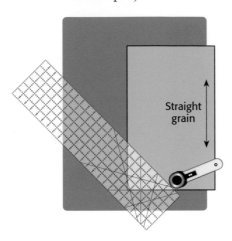

4. Continue cutting strips as usual, measuring from the bias edge.

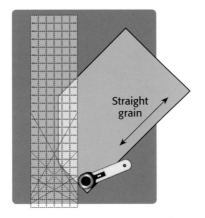

Machine Piecing

With rotary cutting, the pieces are quickly cut and ready to sew. Blocks will soon be flying from your machine!

Set up your machine so that you will be seated comfortably, with your foot able to reach the control pedal. You'll also need a clear view of the presser foot. Have a small pair of scissors or thread snips handy to cut thread ends. Taping a small paper or plastic bag to the table beside your machine is a good way of collecting the snipped thread ends. If possible, have your iron set up close by.

Prepare your machine for straight sewing, setting the stitch length at about 12 stitches per inch, or just under the 2.5 setting.

Sewing Accurate Seam Allowances

The seam allowance for patchwork is ¼" [7.5 mm]. This must be sewn as accurately as it has been cut. If your seam allowance is off by just a little bit, the differences will add up quickly in a block with multiple seams. And remember, ¼" and 7.5 mm are not exactly equivalent and cannot be substituted for each other. If you cut using imperial measurements, then you need to sew that way, too.

There are three ways of setting up your sewing machine for an accurate seam allowance.

Use a ¼" [7.5 mm] foot. The easiest way to maintain an accurate seam allowance is to line up the cut edges of the fabric pieces with the edge of the presser foot. If your machine has a foot with an edge exactly ¼" [7.5 mm] from the needle, you can guide the fabric through the machine by making the cut edges align with the edge of the presser foot. There are special patchwork or ¼" feet for imperial measurements. For metric measurements, some machines have 7.5 mm feet; otherwise, use the methods described below.

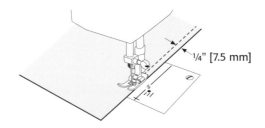

Adjust the needle position. If you don't have a patchwork foot or can't find one for your machine, try adjusting the needle position on your machine so that when you sew there will be exactly ¼" [7.5 mm] between the needle and the edge of the presser foot. To do this, make sure you have a zigzag foot on the machine. (You need a foot with a wide enough opening to accommodate the needle being moved over from center.)

To make the needle position accurate, cut a small piece of graph paper along one of the printed lines. Place the graph paper so that the right edge of the presser foot matches the cut edge of the graph paper. Move the needle sideways so that it will come down exactly on the line that is ¼" [7.5 mm] away from the first line. (Note that for metric graph paper, it will be necessary to mark a 7.5 mm measurement by drawing diagonals across the center of a 5 mm square.)

Important: When you turn off your machine, the needle may revert to the center position. The next time you sew, be sure to reset the needle position.

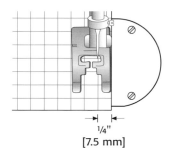

Mark a stitching guide on the machine. If it's not possible for you to use a patchwork foot or to move the machine needle, you can mark a line on the bed of the machine that is exactly ¼" [7.5 mm] from the needle. Using a small piece of graph paper as a guide (as described above), place a strip of masking tape carefully in a straight line next to the edge of the graph paper.

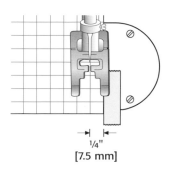

Testing the Seam Allowance

It is vital to spend some time getting the ¼" [7.5 mm] seam allowance right. Your seam allowance may be consistent, but what if it is consistently wrong? Getting it right is worth the trouble.

Test your accuracy by cutting a strip of scrap fabric, 1½" [4 cm] wide. Crosscut the strip to make three rectangles, 1½" x 2½" [4 cm x 6.5 cm]. Sew two of the rectangles together along the longest sides and press the seams to one side. Now take the third rectangle and lay it across the top of the two rectangles. If you did your cutting and stitching correctly, the top rectangle should fit exactly without stretching. If the third rectangle doesn't fit, you'll need to adjust your seam allowance and try again until it does fit exactly.

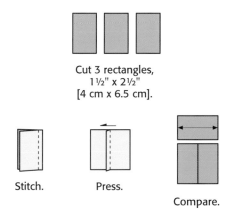

Sewing Pieces Together

Finally, we're ready to start sewing our patchwork!

1. Place the patches right sides together, exactly aligning the edges to be sewn.

2. Place the pieces under the presser foot and lower the presser foot so that the seam will be exactly ¼" [7.5 mm].

3. Sew the length of the seam, keeping the seam allowance exact all the way. Be careful not to let the seam allowance drift and become smaller toward the end of the seam, which is especially easy to do on the corners of triangles.

A wooden toothpick can be used to guide difficult corners. It is not necessary to begin and end with reverse stitching.

4. When you've reached the end of the seam, lift the presser foot, pull your pieces away from the foot, and snip the threads close to the end of your work. Snip away the thread ends at the beginning of your work, too.

5. When sewing triangles together, always trim away the "ears" that are formed at the corners. This will reduce unnecessary bulk in your seam allowances.

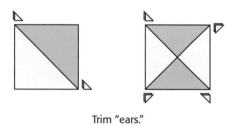

Trim "ears."

NEATNESS COUNTS

Make it a habit to always snip your threads as you go. Your work will be much neater for it, and unwanted threads won't show through your patchwork.

Unpicking a Seam

It happens to all of us—mistakes are made and seams need to be resewn. Use your seam ripper to cut every fifth stitch or so on one side of the seam. Then, using the tip of the seam ripper (turned sideways so it won't cut), gently pull away the thread on the other side of the seam. Remove all bits of thread and press the pieces before resewing.

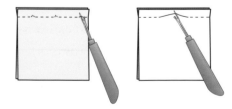

Pressing

For machine piecing to be accurate, each seam must be pressed flat before another seam is sewn across it. Generally, seam allowances are pressed to one side for patchwork, rather than pressed open.

Your first decision is which direction to press the seams. The main goal in pressing is to make the seam allowances nestle neatly in opposite directions at seam junctions. Seam allowances should butt together where they join, with one pair of seam allowances going one way and the opposing set of seam allowances going the other direction. By pressing seams that will later be joined in opposite directions, your patchwork will lie flat and your seam intersections will be accurate.

To easily butt seam allowances, consistently press the seam allowances toward the same fabric when sewing like units. For example, if you are using dark and light squares together to make a Four Patch block, sew the dark and light squares together and press the seams toward the darker fabric. Thus, when the units are joined, the seam allowances will naturally go in opposite directions.

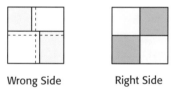

Wrong Side   Right Side

You might also consider pressing toward the darker fabric, to avoid shadows under the light fabric, or pressing seam allowances away from where you plan to do your quilting, because it's easier to stitch through fewer layers of fabric. Where there are several seam allowances together, it is easiest to press them in the direction in which they naturally lie. This can then determine how other neighboring seams should be pressed. The main thing, however, is to press in whatever direction is necessary to make accurate seam junctions, with the seam allowances going in opposite directions.

How to Press

We recommend using steam (or a light spray of water) when pressing pieced seams. While some quilters prefer a dry iron, we believe steam offers advantages. Primarily, steam helps the fabric do what you want it to do. Steam is especially needed when you change your mind about the pressing direction. With all pressing, it is very important not to pull the pieces out of shape. Always press gently, sliding smoothly along. Don't use too vigorous an action.

1. Lay the seamed pieces on your ironing board, but do not open them out. The piece that the seams will be pressed toward should be on top, with the seam farthest away from you.

2. Gently press along the seam to "set the seam." This step is particularly important for pressing bias seams (such as for triangles) to relax any pulling up that may have occurred in the stitching.

3. Open up the patchwork by lifting up the top piece and flipping it away from you so that the sewn patches are both flat and right side up on the ironing board.

4. Gently press the seam flat, taking care not to stretch the seam or press in a fold along the stitching line.

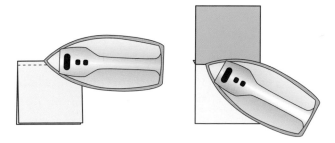

Block Assembly

Patchwork blocks are assembled in a logical way, working from smaller units to larger ones. The pieces or units are then sewn into rows, and finally the rows are sewn together. This approach to block assembly is often called the **piecing order**. Different types of blocks may require different assembly techniques, so work out the piecing order before you begin to sew. The following steps describe the typical sequence used to assemble a block.

1. Lay out your block before sewing. Make sure each piece is in its correct orientation.

2. Sew any smaller pieces together first. Determine which pieces need to be sewn together to form units such as squares or rectangles. When sewing triangles together, always trim away any ears that stick out at the end of the seams. After sewing units within the block, replace them in the layout, and double-check to make sure the design is correct. It's easy to turn parts of the block around and inadvertently create a whole new design!

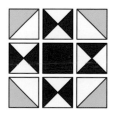   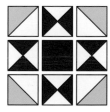

Incorrect   Correct

3. Sew the units together into rows. Press the seams in alternate directions from one row to another—a fundamental process in quiltmaking. That way it is easy to join the rows because adjoining seams will already be pressed in opposite directions. Many quilt diagrams will show arrows indicating which way to press the seams in each row.

4. Sew the rows together. Butt the seam allowances together to make accurate seam junctions. Press seams to one side, and your block is complete.

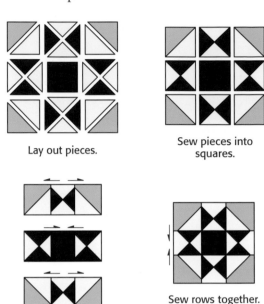

Lay out pieces.

Sew pieces into squares.

Sew squares into rows.

Sew rows together.

Using Pins

Until you gain experience, use pins to help make seam junctions accurate. Place the pieces to be joined with right sides together, aligning the cut edges along the sides you will be sewing together. At the seam junctions, check that seam allowances face opposite directions and use your fingers to feel that the seam allowances are butted together snugly. If they overlap, you'll feel a bump. If they are too far apart, you'll feel a gap. Place pins on either side of the butted seam to hold the join securely, as shown.

Sew the piece together, slowing down as you near the seam junctions. Remove the pins just before you come to them.

If the junctions don't match because one side is a little longer than the other, use pins to help ease in the fullness of the longer side. Pin the two junctions as before, and then place additional pins perpendicular to the edge. Stretch the edge gently as you sew.

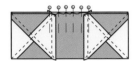

When there are points to be matched in the block, use pins to line up the points accurately before stitching. Do this in three steps:

1. Push a pin through the point, working from the wrong side of the top piece of patchwork.

2. Push the pin through the point of the bottom piece of patchwork, going through from the right side. Keep the pin vertical to the patchwork.

3. Keeping the pieces carefully in place as held by the pin, pin the patches together on each side of the seam junction. Remove the vertical pin and sew the seam.

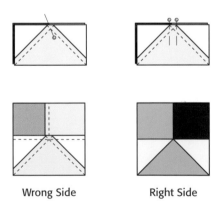

Wrong Side   Right Side

Basic Machine-Piecing Techniques

Rotary cutting and machine piecing lend themselves to all kinds of efficiencies that make creating pieced blocks and quilts even quicker and easier.

Chain-Piecing

Usually in quilting you will not be sewing just one seam, but many seams to make multiple blocks. **Chain-piecing** can make the process quicker because you sew sets of pieces together one after the other, creating a "chain" of units with just a stitch or two of threads between. You save time because you don't stop and start to snip the threads between each set. You also save thread, because you're left with just a small amount to cut away between units.

To chain-piece, feed the pieces under your presser foot as usual, but at the end of each seam take one or two more stitches, and then begin sewing the next set of pieces. When the chain is finished, remove it from the machine, cut off the threads at the beginning and end of the chain, and then snip the threads between each unit. Repeat the chain-piecing process as required for adding additional pieces or units to your blocks.

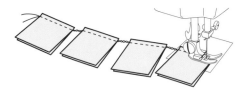

Strip Piecing

Strip piecing is the joining of two or more strips that are then crosscut into units. Many blocks, and units within blocks, consist of squares and rectangles that can be pieced efficiently by first sewing long strips together, pressing the strips flat, and then crosscutting the joined strips into units. Again, you save time by not stopping and starting for each unit.

Strip piecing is especially useful in piecing Four Patch and Nine Patch blocks.

Strip Piecing Four Patch Blocks

1. Cut one strip each from two contrasting fabrics.

2. Join the two strips to make a strip set. Press the seam to one side, generally toward the darker fabric.

3. Square up the end, then crosscut the strip set into segments, cutting the same measurement as the original width of the strip. For example, if strips are cut 2½" [6.5 cm] wide, crosscut into segments 2½" [6.5 cm] wide. From time to time, check that your cuts are at right angles to the strips, and square up as required. This checking and retrimming is necessary because one strip may have stretched a little while it was being sewn.

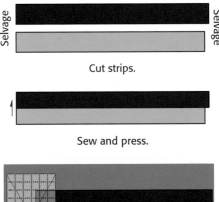

Cut strips.

Sew and press.

Square up end and crosscut into units.

4. Join segments into pairs to make the Four Patch blocks. The seams should nestle together at the seam junction of each Four Patch block. If you are using a directional fabric, be careful to join the segments with the same patch at the top each time, other-

wise the direction of the print will not be the same for all of the blocks.

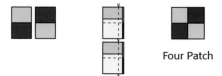

Four Patch

Strip Piecing Nine Patch Blocks

1. From two contrasting fabrics, cut five strips from one fabric and four strips from the other.

2. Join the strips to make three sets of three strips each, alternating the contrasting fabrics, as shown below.

3. Press all seams toward the darker of the two fabrics.

4. Square up the ends, and then crosscut the strip sets into segments, cutting the same measurement as the width of the strips. For example, if strips are cut 2½" [6.5 cm] wide, crosscut into segments 2½" [6.5 cm] wide. From time to time, check that your cuts are at right angles to the strips, and square up as required.

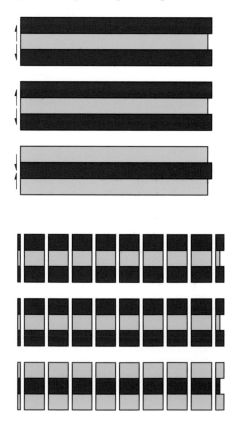

5. Join the units into groups of three to make the Nine Patch block. Because all the seams are pressed toward the same fabric, the units should nestle together neatly at the seam junctions.

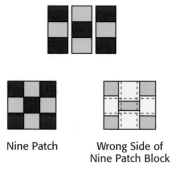

Nine Patch   Wrong Side of
                    Nine Patch Block

Piecing Half-Square-Triangle Units

A **half-square-triangle unit** is a square pieced from two triangles. It is the basis for many patchwork blocks. Sewing individual triangles together is only one way to make this commonly used unit.

Half-Square
Triangle Unit

One of our favorite methods for making half-square-triangle units is to make them in sets of eight using two large squares of fabric. We deliberately add a little extra to the usual measurements to allow for a final trimming, a step we find is worth taking because it results in squares that are completely accurate—and the ears are cut off during the trimming process. To avoid stretching and for even more accuracy, apply a bit of spray starch between the two layers.

1. Lay a piece of fabric on your ironing surface, right side up. Spray this fabric *lightly* with spray starch. Lay a second contrasting fabric onto the first fabric, right side down. Press.

2. Holding the fabrics gently so that they stay together, move fabrics to the cutting mat. Cut a square twice the length of the finished size of the half-square-triangle unit, plus 2½" [7 cm].

For example, if you need half-square-triangle units that finish to 3" [8 cm], cut your starting squares 8½" (3" + 3" + 2½") [23 cm (8 cm + 8 cm + 7 cm)].

3. Using a sharp pencil and your rotary-cutting ruler, mark a line across the diagonal ¼" [7.5 mm] from the center. To mark this line, place the ruler so that the ¼" [7.5 mm] line on the ruler goes exactly from corner to corner of the square. Turn the square around and mark a second diagonal line ¼" [7.5 mm] from the center, as shown. Mark a second pair of lines in the opposite direction.

4. Stitch along the marked lines.

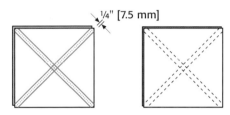

Draw lines and stitch ¼" [7.5 mm] from the diagonals.

5. Press the square flat. Cut the square into four smaller squares by cutting it in half lengthwise through the center. Then, leaving both halves exactly in place, cut in half widthwise, as shown. In our example, we started with 8½" [23 cm] squares, so divide that number in half—4¼" [11.5 cm]—and use that mark on your ruler to make these cuts.

6. Cut between the stitching across the diagonal of each square.

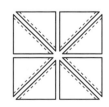

Cut into quarters.   Cut between stitching.

7. Flip open the resulting half-square-triangle units and press the seam allowances toward the same fabric in each unit, usually the darker one.

8. Trim each square to exactly the size required. Remember that this size includes ½" [7.5 mm] for seam allowances. In our example, the size to cut is 3½" [9.5 cm] to get a finished size of 3" [8 cm]. To trim the squares accurately, line up the diagonal line on the ruler exactly with the diagonal seam. Trim two sides, and then flip the square around to trim the remaining two sides.

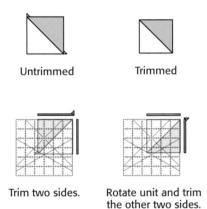

Untrimmed   Trimmed

Trim two sides.   Rotate unit and trim the other two sides.

Piecing Quarter-Square-Triangle Units

A **quarter-square-triangle unit** is a square pieced from four triangles. This unit is found in many blocks.

Quarter-Square-Triangle Unit

Although you can cut individual squares into triangles and sew the triangles together one at a time, the following method efficiently results in pairs of quarter-square-triangle units.

1. From each of two contrasting fabrics, cut a square that is the finished size of the unit plus

1¼" [3.5 cm]. (Remember, that's the magic measurement for quarter-square triangles; see page 42.)

2. Put the squares right sides together with the edges aligned. Using a sharp pencil and your rotary-cutting ruler, mark a line across the diagonal ¼" [7.5 mm] from the center. To mark this line, place the ruler so that the ¼" [7.5 mm] line on the ruler goes exactly from corner to corner of the square.

3. Turn the square around and mark a second diagonal ¼" [7.5 mm] from the other side of the center, as shown.

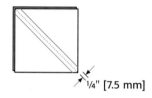

¼" [7.5 mm]

4. Carefully sew along both diagonal lines, sewing on the side of the line toward the block center and just brushing the edge of the line. Sewing next to the line compensates for the slight inaccuracy caused by the distance between the pencil line and the ruler.

5. Cut the squares apart between the two sewn lines, and press the resulting squares open. You will have two half-square-triangle units.

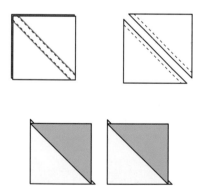

Makes Two Half-Square-Triangle Units

6. Cut each unit across the diagonal opposite to the seam line to make four pieced triangles.

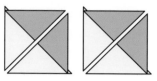

Cut the units on the opposite diagonal.

7. Pair the pieced triangles so that they make quarter-square-triangle units. Note that you'll need to use one pieced triangle from each set so that colors will be opposite one another in the finished units. Place the triangles right sides together, with the center seams butted neatly. It's helpful to pin the seam junctions, as well as the tips of the triangles, especially on larger triangles. Sew the triangles together using a ¼" [7.5 mm] seam allowance. Press the resulting units open and trim away the ears.

Pair triangles to make quarter squares.

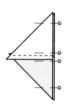

Match seams.   Stitch, press, and trim.

Stitch-and-Fold Corners

Sewing seams on cut bias edges of triangles can lead to stretched seams and misshapen pieces. Quiltmakers have devised a method that lets you sew the seams before cutting the bias angle. Accuracy is improved by stitching through the diagonal center of squares rather than along cut bias edges of triangles. After sewing, the corner is folded open, and the result is a triangle sewn on the corner of the patch—thus the name, **stitch-and-fold corners**.

This method is handy for a variety of common patchwork units, including Flying Geese and Snowball blocks. Look for these units within patchwork blocks—it's surprising how many uses you'll find for this technique.

Admittedly, the stitch-and-fold-corner method does require a little more fabric because some of it gets trimmed away in the end, but most quilters find the improved accuracy is worth it. Besides, instead of wasting the cut-off triangles, you can read our suggestions for using them later. See page 55.

Flying Geese

Snowball

Flying Geese

Traditionally, a flying-geese unit is made by sewing two half-square triangles to the short sides of a larger quarter-square triangle. Here's how to simplify the units using stitch-and-fold corners.

1. Determine the finished size of your flying-geese unit, for example, 3" x 6" [8 cm x 16 cm]. Traditional flying geese are twice as wide as they are tall.

2. For the large center triangles, cut rectangles the finished size of the flying-geese unit plus ½" [1.5 cm]. (Remember, that's the magic measurement for adding seam allowances to rectangles.) For our example, cut rectangles 3½" x 6½" [9.5 cm x 17.5 cm].

3. For each flying-geese unit, cut two squares of background fabric, each measuring the finished height of the flying-geese unit plus ½" [1.5 cm]—the seam allowances for cutting squares. For this example, cut the squares 3½" x 3½" [9.5 cm x 9.5 cm].

4. Using a sharp pencil and a ruler, draw a line on the wrong side of each square going exactly from corner to corner across the diagonal.

5. Place a square and a rectangle right sides together, matching the top left corners and making sure the marked line is positioned as shown. Beginning at the center of the unit, stitch along the diagonal, making the stitching skim along the corner side of the line. By starting to sew at the middle of the rectangle, you give the presser foot more to hold on to than if you'd started at the opposite corner. Remember, sewing next to the line compensates for the slight inaccuracy caused by the distance between the pencil line and the ruler.

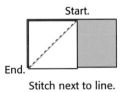

Start.

End.

Stitch next to line.

6. Check accuracy by folding the square over to the corner of the rectangle—the corner of the two pieces should match exactly. Once you're sure it's correct, trim off the excess fabric in the corner, leaving a ¼" [7.5 mm] seam allowance on the side of the stitching closest to the corner. Press the seam flat, and then fold out the corner triangle and press so the seam allowance goes toward the background fabric.

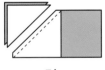

Trim.

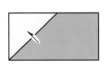

Press.

7. Repeat the process with a second square for the other side of the flying-geese unit, making sure the drawn line starts at the top center and points toward the bottom right corner, as shown.

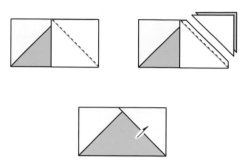

Parallelograms

The stitch-and-fold technique can be varied to make a diamond-shaped parallelogram, which is useful for Star blocks and pieced borders. Instead of sewing the second square in the opposite direction of the first one, sew the stitching line in the same diagonal direction. Note that a left-leaning parallelogram is the reverse of a right-leaning parallelogram, and they are not interchangeable. If you need some of each, you'll need to make some with lines slanting left and some with lines slanting right.

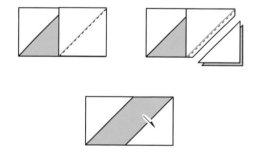

Snowball Blocks

The Snowball block is an octagon with a triangle sewn to each corner. It's easier to make this block by sewing small squares to the corners of a large square using the stitch-and-fold-corner technique than it is to cut an octagon and then sew small triangles along the bias-cut edges.

1. Determine the required finished size of the Snowball block. The Snowball block can be drafted on a nine-patch grid. In our example, we're using a 9" [24 cm] block, where each "patch" in the grid is 3" x 3" [8 cm x 8 cm].

2. For the octagon shape, cut a fabric square that is the finished size of the Snowball block plus ½" [1.5 cm]. In this example, cut a 9½" x 9½" [25.5 cm x 25.5 cm] square.

3. For the corner triangles, cut four squares that are the finished size of the individual "patches" plus ½" [1.5 cm]. For our example, the squares are 3½" x 3½" [9.5 cm x 9.5 cm].

4. Draw a diagonal line from corner to corner across the wrong side of each small square. Working one corner at a time, align a small square with one corner of the large square.

5. Sew the square onto the corner of the larger square, skimming the drawn line on the corner side. Trim away the corner, press the seam flat, and then press the triangle into place, pressing the seam toward the corner.

6. Repeat for each corner.

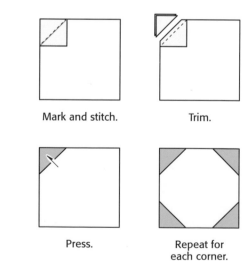

Mark and stitch.   Trim.

Press.   Repeat for each corner.

ALL-STAR SASHING

The stitch-and-fold technique can be used to add small triangles to any corners. For example, eight of these triangles arranged around a central square form a delightful star. See these stars used in sashing in "Piecing Sampler" on page 109.

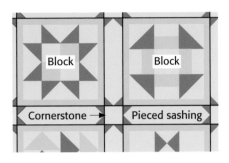

Stitch-and-Fold-Corner Leftovers

Whenever you use the stitch-and-fold technique, you're going to trim away triangles at the corners. Rather than throwing these away, you can sew them together to make little half-square-triangle units, provided the triangles are a reasonable size. These units can be used in making blocks that have little triangle points, such as the Bear's Paw and Kansas Troubles blocks shown below, or for making designs that are made solely of half-square triangles. The Pinwheel and Broken Dishes blocks are good examples.

Pinwheel

Broken Dishes

Bear's Paw

Kansas Troubles

Sew your triangles together as you go so they'll be ready when you need them. Note that the squares may need to be trimmed for accuracy and to fit the size of the new block. You can collect them for a future project, or simply get out the box of these little squares to occupy children when they visit you. They'll enjoy arranging the squares and you'll all be amazed at how many patterns are possible.

Piecing Log Cabin Blocks

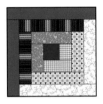

Log Cabin Block

Log Cabin blocks have their own particular construction in that the pieces are sewn together starting at the center of the block and working outward. Traditionally there is a dark square at the center, then half the strips (the "logs") are dark and half the strips are light.

Log Cabin blocks are made entirely from squares and rectangles, so each piece is cut the finished size plus ½" [1.5 cm] for seam allowances.

Because Log Cabin blocks contain many seams, inaccurate sewing will change the size of the block considerably. As a built-in accuracy check, we suggest that you cut each strip to its correct length. As you sew, the length of each strip should match the size of what you have already sewn.

1. Draw the Log Cabin block on graph paper and label each piece with its finished size and cut size (the size with the seam allowances).

2. Cut out the pieces for the block. From a dark fabric, cut out the center square. From both light and dark fabrics, cut strips the required width. Crosscut the strips to make the lengths required.

TIPS FOR LOG CABIN BLOCKS

- When crosscutting strips for Log Cabin blocks, cut the longest strips first. Shorter strips can then be cut from the remainder of the strip.

- Save time by chain-piecing if you are making multiple blocks.

3. Matching cut edges, place the first light strip and the center square right sides together. Sew a seam, being careful to maintain the ¼" [7.5 mm] seam allowance right to the end of the strip; don't "tail off" at the end. Open up the strip and press the seam allowance away from the square. This procedure will be used for adding each strip.

4. Rotate the center square a quarter turn counterclockwise and join the second light strip to the unit made in step 3. If you have sewn and cut accurately, the strip should exactly match. Press the seam allowance toward the newly added strip.

5. Continue to rotate the unit counterclockwise after adding each new strip. Sew the first and second dark strips to the unit. The first round is now complete.

6. Sew the next two light strips to the light side of the block. Note that from now on, you always add a strip to the side that has two seams.

7. Sew the next two dark strips to complete the second round.

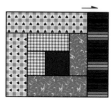 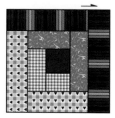

8. Continue in this manner, adding as many rounds as required.

Hand Piecing

Hand piecing in the twenty-first century? Yes! Modern quiltmakers enjoy hand piecing because it is pleasurable, portable, and sociable. The simple, repetitive action of hand sewing is soothing and peaceful. You can work on your patchwork during odd moments and in odd places. Enjoy piecing while chatting with family or friends, watching television, or waiting for appointments.

Hand piecing takes some preparation, but it pays dividends in happy hours of sewing and piles of completed blocks. There is no rule that says if you hand piece some of a quilt, you must do it all by hand. You can hand piece blocks and join them by machine later. Any block in this book can be hand pieced.

KEEPING IT ALL TOGETHER

Keeping your hand-piecing supplies together in a little cloth bag or tin will mean that you are ready to hand piece at any time. For hand piecing, you will need the following: pencil, sharpener, ruler, gridded template plastic, sheet of fine sandpaper (or sandpaper glued to a board), scissors, pins, needle, thimble, and 16" [40 cm] square of fabric, batting, or felt for block layout.

Making Templates

Templates are the pattern shapes used to mark and cut patches. For hand piecing, quiltmakers use a template for each different shape in the block. Templates for hand piecing are made the finished size of the pieces, that is, the size without seam allowances added. You draw around the template shape to mark the hand-stitching lines.

To make templates, draw the block full-size onto gridded template plastic. Cut out one of each shape. Label each shape with its block name and the size of the block. The grain line is indicated by the grid on the plastic.

Aunt Dinah Block

Draw grid.

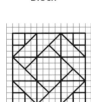

Draw shapes.

Cut out shapes and label.

Marking and Cutting the Fabric

1. Place the fabric, right side down, on top of the sandpaper. The sandpaper will grip the fabric lightly, making it easier to draw the shapes accurately.

2. Place the template, right side down, on top of the fabric. While right side and wrong side won't matter on shapes like squares or rectangles, there are other shapes where it does matter, so it is best to get into the habit of marking with the template right side down. Place the template so that the marked grain line matches the straight grain of the fabric. Place the template so that there is at least ¼" [7.5 mm] of space around the shape.

3. Using a freshly sharpened pencil, hold the template in place and draw lightly around it. Draw as close to the edge of the template as you can, for accuracy. This marked line will be your sewing line. Use a silver pencil for dark fabrics.

4. Repeat for as many shapes as required from that fabric. Be sure to leave at least ½" [1.5 cm] between marked shapes—¼" [7.5 mm] seam allowance for each piece. Repeat the process to mark all the fabrics and shapes needed.

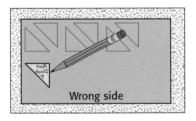

Mark around template.

5. Cut out each shape at least ¼" [7.5 mm] outside the marked line. Cut by eye, as this cutting does not have to be super accurate—your accuracy will come from sewing on the line.

6. Place each piece on the fabric or batting layout square and pin in place. If you place all the

pins horizontally, you can roll the square up for portability.

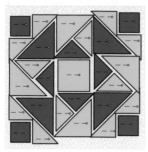

Hand Sewing

1. Take two adjacent pieces from the layout square and put them right sides together. Approximately align the edges on the side you are about to sew.

2. Pin the pieces together so that they are ready for sewing. Push a pin through the top piece at the end of the sewing line; then push the pin through the right side of the lower piece, checking on the wrong side to make sure it is accurately at the end of the line. Repeat at the other end of the sewing line.

3. Anchor pins by taking a small "bite" into the fabric pieces, with the pins at right angles or perpendicular to the sewing line. Pinching each end in either hand, gently tug the pieces horizontally to align the marked lines on both sides. Pin the center. Check that you pinned accurately along the line on both sides. Add more pins for long seams.

4. Cut a piece of thread about 12" [30 cm] long, thread it onto your needle, and tie a knot at one end.

HOW TO TIE A KNOT

- Place the end of the thread over your fingertip and cross the thread end with the threaded needle.

- Wrap the thread gently twice around the needle (more wraps will make a larger knot, if desired).

- Pinch the wraps gently with your forefinger and thumb and pull needle through until the knot is firm.

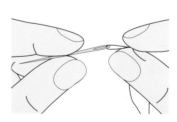

5. Begin stitching about ¼" [7.5 mm] from the end of the marked sewing line, as shown. Stitch toward the corner, remove the corner pin, and then stitch exactly into the corner.

Note that you can sew from left to right or right to left, as you prefer.

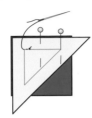

6. Change direction and sew a running stitch exactly on the line, removing pins as you go. Stitch exactly into the corner, change direction, and take a couple of small stitches back toward the center. Then take two small stitches on the same spot to anchor the thread and snip off the remaining thread. The backstitching at the beginning and end of the seam strengthens the ends of the seam—if you began and ended the stitching at the ends of the line, the corners would be weaker.

7. Continue stitching pieces together in the same manner. Any patch can be added to any adjacent patch; there is no special order to follow as with machine piecing.

8. When crossing seams, do not sew across the seam allowances as with machine piecing. The seam allowances should be allowed to stick up, free of stitching. Sew only on the drawn lines.

Leave seam allowances free.

9. Press the whole block after it is completed. Press seams to one side, alternating the sides at seam junctions.

10. If you intend to join blocks by machine, trim the finished block exactly square and to the size required using your rotary cutter and large square ruler. The correct size is the finished block size plus ¼" [7.5 cm] all around for seam allowances. If you join blocks by hand you will match up the seam lines, not the outer edges, making this trimming step unnecessary.

Hand-piecing supplies ready to go

Appliqué

Appliqué is the sewing of patches onto a background fabric. Unlike piecing, which is typically made with geometric shapes, appliqué lets you work with all sorts of shapes. From realistic flower motifs to simplistic folk-art shapes to contemporary forms, appliqué gives you freedom in design.

Hand Appliqué

The essence of good hand appliqué is in the preparation of the shapes that you will appliqué to the background. There are numerous methods for preparing pieces, but we find that using spray starch works best, because the starch enables you to sculpt the fabric around the appliqué template. This results in perfect shapes that are completely ready for stitching. Once the pieces are prepared, your hand appliqué will be quite portable.

Getting Ready

You'll need the following materials to prepare the appliqué shapes and begin stitching: spray starch, glass jar with lid, small craft paintbrush, dressmaking pins, sharp scissors, iron, square of scrap fabric to protect ironing surface, template plastic and lightweight card stock or manila folder for templates, fine-point permanent marker, sharp pencil, hand-sewing needle, and thread.

1. Spray the starch into the jar. It will foam up at first, and then settle into a clear liquid. (Note that the liquid starch keeps well, and can be stored in the lidded jar.)

> ### THREADS FOR HAND APPLIQUÉ
> For appliqué, it is important to use threads that match the pieces to be appliquéd, not the background. If you match the color closely, your stitches will be almost invisible. Many different colors of thread may be required. For example, for a yellow flower with green leaves, you may need several different shades of yellow as well as green thread.

2. Cover your ironing surface with a piece of scrap fabric.

3. Cut out the background square for appliqué, cutting it to the finished size of the block plus

1" [3 cm] all around for seam allowances. This extra-wide seam allowance will allow you to trim the block to precisely the right size after all the appliqué is finished.

4. Fold the background square into quarters and mark the center by lightly creasing the folds.

Fold in half and crease
to mark center.

Preparing an Appliqué Shape

1. Draw or trace the appliqué shape onto the template plastic using the fine-point permanent marker. Copy any markings such as numbers or center points. Cut out the shape, making sure both curved and straight edges are smooth by rotating the plastic through the scissors as you gently close them—that is, move the plastic around rather than the scissors. The plastic shape becomes your master template. (Only use the plastic template to make the card-stock templates. Do not use the iron on the plastic template; it will melt.)

2. Place the plastic shape on top of the card stock and draw around it with pencil. Carefully cut out the card-stock shape as described in step 1.

3. Mark the wrong side of the card-stock template with WS to indicate wrong side. If required, mark the center point by piercing a pin through the card.

4. With the wrong side of the template facing up, pin the template onto the wrong side of the

fabric. Cut out the shape, allowing an approximate ¼" [6 mm] seam allowance all around.

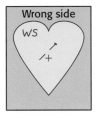 

¼" [6 mm]
seam allowance

5. Lay the appliqué shape on your ironing surface, right side down, with the template in place on the fabric. Paint the spray starch around the seam allowance using the paintbrush. The seam allowance should be wet, but not dripping.

6. With your iron set on medium heat and no steam, press the seam allowance back over the template, gradually working around the shape. Begin pressing on a straight or gently curved side. Use your fingers to fold the seam allowance gently over the template while smoothing the fabric with the tip of the iron. Gently hold the iron in place until the fabric is dry and that segment of the seam allowance is set. Repeat these actions around the shape. See the next section for coping with curves, points, and corners.

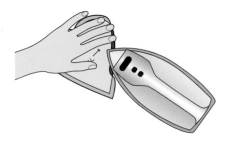

7. When the seam allowance is pressed all around the shape, turn the shape over and press from the right side. Leave the template inside the shape until you are ready to sew.

Working with Curves and Points

Convex curves. For these curves, which curve outward like a circle, make small pleats in the seam allowance as your fingers pull it back, to take up the excess fabric.

Make pleats around convex curves.

Concave curves. For these curves, which curve inward as if a bite has been taken out of a shape, make small snips into the seam allowance so that it can lie flat and smooth over the template edge. Use just the tip of your scissors to make the cuts, to be sure you cut a little short of the template edge.

Snip concave curves.

Inner corners. For inner corners, such as the inside of a V shape, make a cut into the seam allowance, cutting almost into the corner. This will enable you to press the seam allowance flat on either side of the corner.

Snip inner corners.

Outer corners. For outer corners, such as the corners of squares, fold the seam allowance in two stages. First, fold the seam allowance over one side of the template, folding it beyond the edge of the template, right up to the end of the fabric. Next, fold over the folded seam allowance at the corner, and press.

First Fold   Second Fold

Narrow points. For sharp points, fold the seam allowance in three stages. First, fold the seam allowance at the point straight back over the template. Next, fold the seam allowance over one long side. Finally, fold the seam allowance over the second side. Press. Tuck in any excess.

First Fold   Second Fold   Third Fold

Preparing Special Shapes

Bias strips. For long narrow shapes, such as stems and basket handles, cut a bias strip three times the width of the finished appliqué and ½" [1.5 cm] longer than the required length to account for seam allowances at each end. (See "Cutting Bias Strips" on page 43.)

Finger-fold the strip into thirds along the length and hand baste the layers together along the center of the strip with a running stitch. Do not press the strip with the iron, as you do not want to lock the strip into a final shape at this time. Pin and appliqué the strip in place. The ends of the strip can be tucked under another shape or folded under and sewn neatly.

Circles. To make an appliqué circle, cut the template out of card stock as with any other shape. Cut the fabric ¼" [7.5 mm] larger than the template.

Thread your needle and tie a knot in the thread. Sew a small running stitch around the circle, ⅛" [3 mm] from the cut edge, beginning and ending on the right side of the fabric.

Place the template on the wrong side of the fabric circle and pull the thread to gather the fabric firmly around the template. Pull on both the knotted end and the loose thread end. Tie off the thread securely. Steam press, or dampen the seam allowance with spray starch and press. Snip the thread and undo the running stitch. Remove the template and press the circle again from the right side. For very small circles, such as those used for berries, you may need to trim away the excess seam allowance.

Sewing the Appliqués

1. Remove the template from the prepared appliqué shape and place the shape on the background fabric. Use the center mark on the template to help with placement, if appropriate. Pin the shape in place.

2. Turn the background over and pin the appliqué again from the wrong side. Then you can remove the pins from the right side. By pinning from the wrong side you won't have pins sticking out that will invariably catch your thread as you sew.

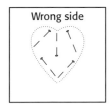

Pin from wrong side.

3. Thread a needle with a length of thread to match the appliqué fabric. Tie a knot at the end of the thread (see page 58).

4. To hide the knot, bring the needle up from the wrong side of the appliqué, through the edge of the seam allowance. The knot will then be in the fold of the appliqué rather than on the back of the work. Begin stitching the appliqué along a straight edge or one that is just slightly curved.

5. Take a very small stitch back down into the background fabric, as close as possible to where the thread comes out of the appliqué. Bring the needle back up again at an angle, coming through both the background fabric and the appliqué edge about ⅛" [3 mm] from the first stitch. This will result in a very small stitch on the right side of your work, where it's holding the appliqué shape in place, and a stitch just less than ⅛" [3 mm] on the wrong side of the block, where the thread travels along to the next stitch. Continue stitching in this manner around the shape.

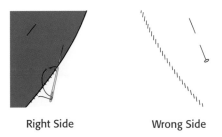

Right Side   Wrong Side

6. When stitching into an inside corner, make stitches closer together on each side of the snipped point, and make one stitch with a slightly larger bite right into the corner. The larger stitch will help secure the inner point where there is no seam allowance to stitch into.

7. End the stitching on the wrong side of the block with a couple of small backstitches. Then travel the needle and thread between the background and appliqué for a short distance, bring the needle out, and snip off the thread.

Appliquéing Multiple Pieces

For a design that has several overlapping appliqué shapes, it is important to decide in what order the various shapes need to be sewn. Number each piece according to the sewing order.

Any part of a seam allowance that will be covered by another shape on top does not need to be turned under. Not only will it be hidden by the appliqué on top, but by not turning it under you will also reduce its bulk. To indicate which seam allowances do not need to be turned under, mark the template with a zigzag line as a reminder to leave them flat.

1. Trace the entire appliqué design onto the background fabric using a sharp pencil. Trace very lightly, drawing the line so that it skims along just inside the line for each shape. For a dark background, use a silver pencil and tape the design and the fabric to a window. Number each piece by stitching sequence. Match the center mark on the design with the center of the background.

2. Trace the design onto your template plastic, marking the numbers, a cross for the center of the design, and the zigzag lines that indicate where pieces will overlap. Cut the design apart to make the individual templates. Draw around each shape onto card stock, transfer-

ring markings and numbers onto the wrong side. Carefully cut out each shape.

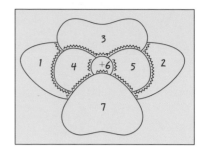

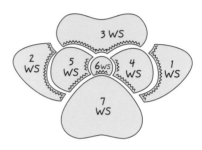

3. Prepare each appliqué shape, referring to "Preparing an Appliqué Shape" on page 61. However, remember to leave the seam allowances unstarched and unpressed along the sides of the templates marked with zigzag lines.

4. Beginning with the first piece, slip out the template and match the piece to its number on the background fabric. Pin the appliqué in place, as in steps 1 and 2 of "Sewing the Appliqués" on page 63. Appliqué the piece in place, starting where the shape will be overlapped by a later piece and working your way around.

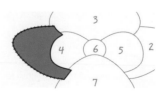

5. Add pieces in numerical order, taking out the templates before pinning and stitching. The last piece you add will always have its seam allowances pressed under on all edges.

6. When all the pieces are appliquéd, press the block, and then trim the block to the required size (finished size plus ¼" [7.5 mm] seam allowances all around the block) using your rotary cutter and large square ruler. Remember to trim evenly from all four sides so that your design will still be centered in the block after trimming.

Machine Appliqué

If you prefer stitching by machine or you want to make an appliqué project quickly, machine appliqué may suit you. Fusible web enables you to adhere shapes to background fabrics ready for stitching. Modern machines are able to do beautiful satin stitching, blanket stitching, or other decorative stitching to finish the appliqué edges.

Getting Ready

You will need your sewing machine, paper and fabric scissors, iron, a small piece and a large piece of nonstick baking parchment (to protect your iron and ironing board from glue), lightweight fusible web with paper backing, machine embroidery thread, bobbin fill or fine cotton thread, a stabilizer such as copier paper, and template plastic.

It's a good idea to clean and oil your machine before starting a machine appliqué project. Set up your machine with a size 70 embroidery needle and attach the embroidery or open-toe presser foot.

Preparing Shapes with Fusible Web

1. Draw or trace the appliqué shapes onto template plastic. You need only one template of each shape. Label the right side of each template.

2. Place the template, right side down, on top of the paper side of the fusible web. Draw around the shape. Cut out the shape roughly, cutting about ¼" [7.5 mm] outside the drawn shape.

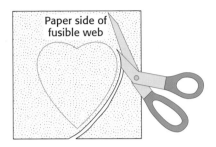

3. Cover your ironing surface with the large piece of baking parchment. Place the appliqué fabric, wrong side up, on top of the parchment. Place the fusible web shape on top, paper side up. Cover with the small piece of baking parchment. With your iron on the cotton setting and using no steam, press according to the directions on the fusible web. If you press too long, chances are the web won't stick well.

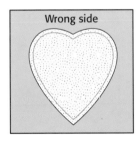

4. Cut out the appliqué shape precisely on the drawn line.

5. Remove the paper backing from the shape. Gently use a pin to pry the layers apart, taking care not to stretch the fabric edges.

6. Lay the background fabric right side up on the ironing board. Place the prepared appliqué exactly in place and cover it with a small sheet of baking parchment. Press according to the fusible web directions.

7. When all appliqués have been fused in place, pin the appliqué block on top of a piece of stabilizer.

Machine Stitching the Shapes

As we mentioned earlier, you have a few options when it comes to adding the machine stitching. In describing the technique, we'll focus on satin stitching. However, you may want to experiment with other decorative stitches, such as blanket stitching or featherstitching.

It is essential to practice your stitching on a scrap piece of fabric to make sure that your stitch width and length, as well as your thread tension, are appropriate. Then you can move on to your actual appliqué block.

1. Set your sewing machine for a narrow zigzag stitch. Thread the machine with embroidery thread on the top and fine cotton thread or bobbin fill in the bobbin.

2. On a scrap of fabric, test to get the right settings for satin stitching. Use stabilizer beneath the fabric to prevent puckering and keep the satin stitch from lumping up. Set the stitch at the width desired, then experiment with the stitch length until the satin stitch is smooth and flat, with the threads lying next to each other. If the stitch length is too short, the threads will bunch up on top of one another. If the length is too long, the stitches will have spaces between them. Only the top thread should show, with no bobbin thread coming through. If the bobbin thread is pulling up to the top, loosen the top thread tension on your machine.

3. To begin stitching your actual appliqué block, position it under the machine so that the needle will come down just outside the appliqué shape. When the needle swings to the other side of the zigzag, it should go into the appliqué fabric. Do not begin at a corner, but rather choose a side with a straight line or a smooth curve.

4. Working the machine by hand, bring the needle down and up through the fabric so that the bobbin thread comes up in a loop. Pull gently on the bobbin thread until the end comes out of the machine. Lay both top and bottom threads straight in front of the presser foot and hold them in place with your thumb or finger. (Don't hold them too tightly, as they need to slide under your finger as the sewing begins.)

5. Take five or six stitches, making sure the stitches cover the thread ends. Stop sewing and cut off the thread ends that still extend beyond the stitching.

6. Continue stitching around the shape, letting the machine move the fabric through the presser foot, but gently guiding the direction of the sewing as required.

7. To end satin stitching, sew until the satin stitch meets the beginning stitch, finishing with the needle up and the thread coming from the inside of the satin stitch. Change the stitch width to straight stitching, keeping the stitch length very short. Move the appliqué so that the needle will be at the inside edge of the satin stitch and take several stitches to lock the

threads in place. Snip the threads close to the stitching.

8. Tear away the stabilizer from inside and outside the appliqué shape. (Due to the stitching it may already be removed.) You do not have to take out the little bit of paper caught in the satin stitch itself. Press the finished piece.

9. If your pattern has more than one shape, fuse all the pieces in place and then stitch around just the edges that are visible.

MANEUVERING CURVES AND POINTS

When you come to a tight curve, stop sewing with the needle down on the outside of the curve. Note that you always stop on the outside of the curve. Sometimes this will mean stopping with the needle on the inside of the appliqué shape, and sometimes it will mean stopping with the needle in the background fabric outside the appliqué, depending on whether your appliqué shape has a concave or convex curve.

Lift the presser foot to turn the appliqué slightly, lower the presser foot, and continue sewing. Repeat this pivoting as often as required for the shape, which may mean as often as every few stitches.

To make a neat corner, stitch right to the edge of the corner as shown, finishing with the needle down at the point of the corner. Lift the presser foot and swivel the appliqué so you are ready to stitch the next side of the point. Raise the needle and move the appliqué very slightly so that the needle will come down just inside the outer edge of the previous stitching. Continue stitching as before.

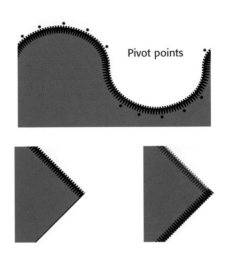

Pivot points

Quilt Assembly

Once you have your patchwork or appliqué blocks finished,

it's time to assemble them into the quilt.

Quilt Layout

Laying out the quilt is the important initial step. Use a design wall if you have one, or any clear space such as a floor, or even the top of your bed. The layout step serves two purposes. First, it gives you a chance to place everything in position so that you can join the pieces in a correct order. Second, it allows you to take a final look at how the quilt is working as a whole. It's not too late to make some changes.

Lay out the blocks and any sashing and cornerstones, checking that all the blocks are positioned correctly. If blocks are made from different prints, check that the colors are distributed across the quilt. You don't want all the blocks with the same prints too close together.

Now look at the quilt from as much distance as you can. If you can't step back very far, try looking through a camera lens or door peephole. Viewing the quilt from a distance will help you spot anything you might want to change.

Quilt-Top Assembly

Elements of a quilt are sewn together in the same logical way that blocks are put together: the blocks are sewn into rows, and then the rows are sewn together.

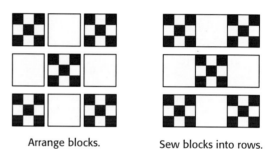

Arrange blocks.   Sew blocks into rows.

Sew rows together.

When sewing the rows of blocks together, always pin the junctions of the blocks, so that the blocks will be accurately aligned (see "Using Pins," page 48).

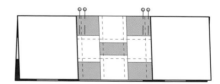

It can be helpful to label the rows by pinning a number onto the first block in each row (the block in the left-most column). We like to put a period after the number so that we can easily tell in which direction the blocks should be turned. Some numbers, such as 1, 6, and 9, can be easily turned the wrong way up!

Carefully collect the blocks into a stack, taking them in order from one end of the row so that the numbered block comes out on top. Take one stack at a time to your machine and sew the blocks together, keeping them in the correct order and orientation.

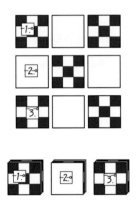

Adding Sashing Strips

If your quilt has sashing strips, sew the sashing strips and cornerstones into rows in the same manner as for the blocks.

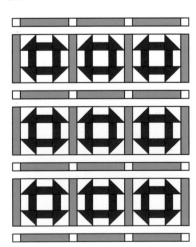

Sometimes sashing is used without cornerstones. In this case, the blocks in each horizontal row are separated by short sashing strips. Then between the rows of blocks, you'll have long sashing strips that go from side to side of the quilt.

Make this type of sashing as follows.

1. Cut the short vertical sashing strips the same length as the quilt block, including seam allowances. Sew the sashing strips and blocks into a row.

2. Measure and cut the long horizontal sashing strips so they are the same width as the row of blocks and vertical sashing strips joined, including the seam allowances on each side.

3. Mark these strips with pins, or with a pencil on the wrong side of the fabric, to show the junctions that must match. Join the rows, matching seam junctions with the pins or markings.

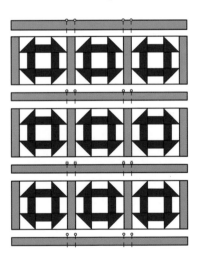

Pressing Rows

Just as with making blocks, pressing is very important for quilt assembly. You'll want the seam allowances to go in opposite directions at each seam junction, making the joins accurate. Wherever possible, press seam allowances in the directions they naturally lie. In quilt instructions, the direction to press the seams is often indicated by arrows.

When your quilt is made of pieced blocks that are sewn together with no sashing or alternate blocks in between, press all the seams in one row in one direction and all the seams in the next row in the opposite direction. Continue alternating seam directions from row to row.

When you have alternate plain blocks, it's easiest to press the seams toward the plain blocks. This is also true for quilts with sashing strips. Pressing this way reduces bulk, as you're not folding back multiple layers of patchwork.

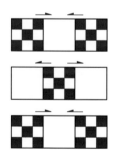

Assembling Diagonal-Set Quilts

Quilts with the blocks set diagonally are sometimes called **"on-point"** quilts. This type of quilt is also assembled in rows. However, you need to finish off what would otherwise be jagged edges with what we call **setting triangles**.

Arrange blocks.   Sew blocks into rows.

Sew rows together.

Typically, large quarter-square triangles are used along the side, top, and bottom edges, and half-square triangles are used at the quilt corners. All the triangles along the quilt edges are cut so that the straight of grain runs along the edge of the quilt.

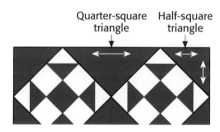

Setting triangles need straight grain on outer edges.

To determine how large to cut the side setting triangles, you need to know the diagonal measurement of the block size in your quilt. One way to determine this is to measure the diagonal of the finished block—that is, the block without seam allowances. Either draw a square the size of the block or use the grid on your cutting mat. Measure exactly across the diagonal of the square and round up the measurement to the nearest ⅛" [5 mm]. Then add the seam allowance for cutting quarter-square triangles, which is 1¼" [3.5 cm].

The other way to determine the diagonal measurement is quicker, provided you have a calculator handy. Multiply the finished block size (again, without seam allowances) by 1.41. Round up the answer to the nearest ⅛" [5 mm] and add 1¼" [3.5 cm] the seam allowance for cutting quarter-square triangles. For example, the calculation for a 9" [25 cm] block looks like this:

1. 9" x 1.41 = 12.69" [24 cm x 1.41 = 33.84 cm].

2. Round that up to 12¾" [34 cm].

3. 12¾" + 1¼" = 14" [34 cm + 3.5 cm = 37.5 cm].

Cut squares to this size and then cut the squares across both diagonals to make four triangles per square.

To determine what size to cut the corner triangles, divide the diagonal measurement in half. Again round up the measurement to the nearest ⅛" [5 mm]. Add the seam allowance for cutting half-square triangles, which is ⅞" [2.5 cm]. Again, using a 9" [25 cm] block as an example, the calculation looks like this:

1. 12¾" ÷ 2 = 6⅜" [34 cm ÷ 2 = 17 cm].

2. 6⅜" + ⅞" = 7¼" [17 cm + 2.5 cm = 19.5 cm].

Cut two squares to this size and then cut the squares in half diagonally to make four corner triangles.

At the back of the book, we give a list of cutting sizes for half-square triangles and quarter-square triangles for common block sizes (see page 158).

CROSSWISE VS. LENGTHWISE BORDERS

Border strips can be cut across the width of the fabric or along the length. Often, cutting the borders across the width saves fabric. If your quilt is longer than your fabric is wide, you will need to sew two or more strips together to make the lengths required.

Join the strips by first squaring up their ends. Then stitch two ends together using a ¼" [7.5 mm] seam allowance. We recommend that you press the seam open to reduce bulk.

Stitch.   Press seam open.

Allow extra fabric if you want to match a design, but don't be obsessive about a perfect match unless this is a really important feature of the quilt. You are making a patchwork quilt, after all. If the borders are patched, they'll just be part of the patchwork look. For a look at borders that are pieced, see "Lion Around" on page 130.

To match a stripe or print on border strips, mark the point that matches on each strip. Cut a ¼" [7.5 mm] seam allowance beyond these points, and then sew the strips together. Make joins less visible by cutting in the background area of a print.

If your border fabric is a directional print or if the seams will be very visible, you may want to cut long borders on the lengthwise grain. See page 43 for directions on cutting lengthwise down the fabric.

Adding Borders

Always look at a border fabric next to your quilt top before you begin cutting and sewing. What seemed to be the perfect border fabric in the quilt shop may not be the perfect one in the end. If you haven't decided on borders, audition various fabrics by pinning or holding them up next to the quilt top.

A quilt may have just one border, or two, or even more borders. Often a narrow border strip of an accent color can really bring a quilt to life.

One Border   Two Borders

Another option to consider for your borders is how you'll treat the corners. The corners can be butted, mitered, or finished off with an added square. We'll cover each of these options in the following sections.

Butted Corner   Mitered Corner

Corner Square

Fitting Borders

The essential concept for borders is that they must be made so that the quilt is both flat and a proper square or rectangle. To achieve this, the borders on opposite sides of the quilt must be exactly the same measurement; this measurement is determined by measuring the quilt through its center. To measure for side borders, measure the center length of the quilt top. To measure for the top and bottom borders, measure across the center width of the quilt top.

If you sew strips of fabric to the sides of the quilt without measuring, the quilt top may stretch as you sew, and you will end up with wavy borders and a quilt that will not lie flat or hang straight.

Measure through the center.

Pin marking is a technique used to fit borders evenly to the quilt top. Pin marking involves using pins to mark points on a border and on the quilt that will be matched up as you attach the borders. Fold the border strip in half and mark the center with a pin. Then fold it into quarters to mark the midpoints of each half. Do the same for your quilt top. Match the pin marks when pinning on the borders. Because the center length of the quilt can differ a bit from the outer edge lengths, either your cut borders or your quilt top may need to be eased to fit together. Pin marking helps to distribute evenly any extra length on the border or quilt top as you sew the two pieces together.

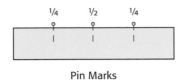

Pin Marks

Butted Corners

The simplest way to add borders to a quilt is to use butted corners. Border strips are sewn to the sides of the quilt, and then strips are sewn to the top and bottom of the quilt, including the side borders in the process.

1. For side borders, cut strips a little longer than the measurement of the sides of the quilt top; about 1" [2.5 cm] longer is adequate.

2. Trim one end of each strip so that it is square.

3. Lay out the quilt center in a clear, flat space. Smoothly lay the strips down the center of the quilt top, with the squared ends exactly matching the top edge of the quilt. Take care not to stretch the border as you smooth it out. Make a small snip with the scissors at the ends of the border strips where they match the bottom edge of the quilt top.

Squared-up ends

Snip.

4. Cut the border strips square, using the small snip as a guide. Fold the border strips in half and pin mark the centers. Fold again to mark quarter lengths, and pin mark the points.

5. Pin mark the center of each side of the quilt by folding the quilt top in half both lengthwise and widthwise. Fold again, and pin mark the quarter points.

Pin mark.

6. Pin the strips to the sides of the quilt, matching the pin marks and matching the ends of the borders with the top and bottom edges of the quilt. Pin the rest of the border to the quilt top by continuing to place pins midway between the pins you have already placed. Then pin at the midway of each of those newly created spaces, and so on. You may have to slightly stretch or ease the borders sometimes, as the edges of the quilt top may have stretched with handling. Keep pinning in the middle of the spaces until the border has pins about 2" [5 cm] apart, so that any excess fabric in the quilt top is evenly pinned to the border.

7. Sew the border strips to the sides of the quilt. Press the seam allowances toward the borders.

8. Measure the width of the quilt through the center (including the side borders you've just added) and cut top and bottom border strips a little longer than this measurement. Trim one end of the border strips square; then lay the strips across the center of the quilt top. Make a small snip in the border strips to mark where the border strips match the side edges of the quilt.

Snip to mark edge.

9. Trim the border strips square as you did for the side borders, using the small cut as a guide. Pin mark the border strips and quilt top into quarters.

10. Pin the borders to the top and bottom of the quilt as for the side borders. Sew the strips to the quilt and press toward the border. If there are multiple borders, complete each border in the same manner before adding the next border.

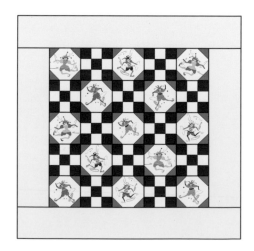

Corner Squares

For an added decorative touch, you can sew corner squares to borders. The process for making the borders is the same as for butted corners, above, with a slight variation.

1. Measure through the center of your quilt top to determine the correct length of your border strips, matching the side borders to the quilt length and the top and bottom borders to the quilt width. Cut borders to these lengths.

2. Cut the corner squares the same size as the width of the border. For example, for a finished 6" [15 cm] border, cut the border strips 6½" [16.5 cm] wide and cut the corner squares 6½" x 6½" [16.5 cm x 16.5 cm].

3. Join the side borders to the sides of the quilt as explained in "Butted Corners" on page 73. Join the squares to each end of the top and bottom border strips and press the seam allowances toward the border strips. Sew the strips to the quilt, matching the seams at the corners of the quilt.

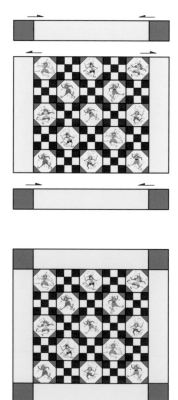

Mitered Corners

Borders with **mitered corners** are joined with a diagonal seam at the corners. Use mitered corners for borders of stripes or prints so that the pattern meets nicely in the corners.

1. Cut border strips the length of the quilt top, plus twice the border width, plus 2" [5 cm]. For example, if the quilt is 50" [125 cm] long and the borders will be 6" [15 cm] wide, cut the border strips 50" + 12" + 2" = 64" [125 cm + 30 cm + 5 cm = 160 cm] long. If the quilt is square, all border strips will be the same length. If the quilt is rectangular, the measurements for the side borders will be different from the top and bottom borders.

2. Fold and pin mark the center of each border strip. Pin mark the center of each side of the quilt.

3. Lay out the quilt top in a clear, flat space. Lay the border strips for the sides of the quilt lengthwise along the quilt top, matching the center of the quilt with the center pin marks of the strips. Pin mark the strips at each end, parallel to the edge of the quilt.

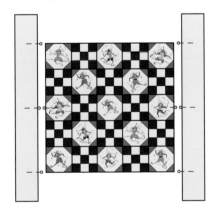

4. On the wrong side of the fabric, use a pencil to mark a point on the seam line exactly ¼"

[7.5 mm] in from the pin marks at each end of the strips.

¼" seam

5. Pin the strips to the quilt, matching the center pin marks and the ends of the quilt with the pin marks on the strips.

6. Sew the strips to the quilt, beginning and ending by backstitching at the marked points ¼" [7.5 mm] from the edges of the quilt top. It is very important to stitch exactly to these points. Press the seam allowances toward the border.

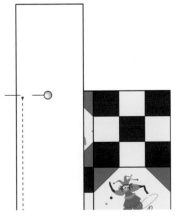

Stitch only to marked point.

7. Repeat this process for the top and bottom borders, but measuring widthwise through the center of the quilt. Again, sew only to your marked end points.

8. To miter the corner, fold the quilt top in half diagonally, right sides together. Carefully align the long edges of two adjacent borders. At the corner, temporarily fold the border seam allowances toward the center of the quilt. Using the 45° line on your quilting ruler, mark each border strip on the wrong side with a line going from the end of the stitching to the edge of the border, as shown.

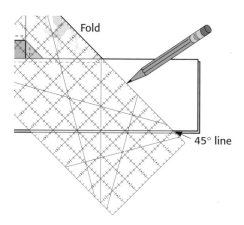

9. Pin the two strips together, matching the lines carefully as you go. Sew the strips together to form the miter, beginning exactly at the inside corner and sewing toward the outside corner of the border. As you stitch, keep the border seam allowances turned toward the quilt center to avoid catching them in the seam.

10. After checking on the right side of your quilt to make sure the miter is smooth, trim away the excess fabric, leaving a ¼" [7.5 mm] seam allowance. Press the seam open. Repeat for the remaining three corners.

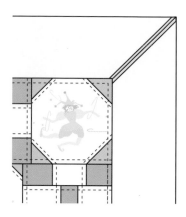

MITERING MULTIPLE BORDERS

If your quilt has more than one border and you want to miter the corners, sew the individual border strips together first. Then add them to the quilt as a single unit. When sewing the corners, make sure the edges of the strips match up for a perfect miter of each one of your borders.

Join strips together.

Hand and Machine Quilting

As the saying goes, "It is not a quilt until it is quilted."

Quilting stitches not only hold the three layers of the quilt together but also add texture and beauty to the surface of the quilt. The quilting creates lines, compressing the quilt layers and creating little hills and valleys that make light and shadow play delightfully across the quilt.

Assembling the Layers

Before you can start quilting, you need to make the quilt backing and then layer and baste the backing, batting, and quilt top together.

Preparing the Backing

Choose a backing fabric that will suit the color and style of your quilt. The back of your quilt should be a nice surprise when the quilt is turned over, not something that doesn't fit the character of your quilt. Generally, fabric for backing is calculated from the size of the quilt top plus 4" [10 cm], which gives about 2" [5 cm] all around the quilt top for insurance. Here we describe how to make a backing from a single fabric, but it is also possible to sew various fabrics together to make a backing. You might want to try this to add interest or simply to use up odds and ends of fabric. The various fabrics need to be sewn together to reach the required size. Press all seams open.

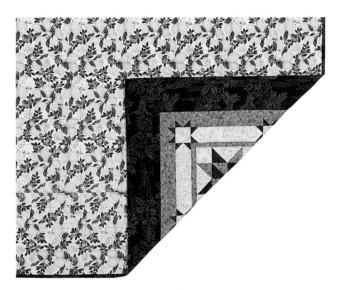

Back of "Lemons and Blueberries" (shown on page 109).

Back of "Cabin in the Garden" (shown on page 139).

1. To determine the amount of backing fabric you'll need, calculate the width and length of the finished quilt top plus 4" [10 cm]. The usable amount of fabric is generally about 40" [100 cm] wide. So, if your quilt is wider than 36" [90 cm] you'll need more than one length of fabric for the backing. Depending on the size of your quilt, it is sometimes most fabric-efficient to piece the backing segments together with a horizontal seam across the center. At other times a lengthwise seam makes more sense. Determine how many lengths or widths of fabric you need, then add an extra 2" [5 cm] to allow for shrinkage and crooked cutting.

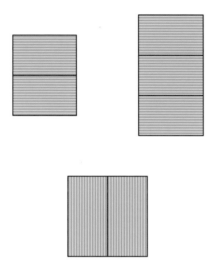

2. Cut away the selvage edges of the backing fabric, as they are more tightly woven than the rest of the fabric and cause puckering.

3. Cut the backing fabric into as many lengths as required and sew the lengths together. Press these seams open.

4. Trim the backing as needed, so that it will be 4" [10 cm] larger than the quilt. Trim the batting to the same size as the backing.

5. For small quilts that are just over 40" [100 cm] wide, you can cut two strips from the backing fabric and join these to add to the sides of the length of backing, as shown.

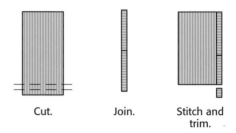

Cut.   Join.   Stitch and
                          trim.

Layering

Layering is the process of assembling the quilt sandwich so it will be ready for quilting. The quilt sandwich consists of the backing on the bottom, the batting in the middle, and the quilt top on top. Layering is best done in a large, flat space, on the biggest table you can manage (a table-tennis table is ideal), or else on the floor. Don't layer on a precious surface, as the pins will scratch.

1. Spread out the prepared backing, right side down. Use masking tape to adhere the backing to the floor or table surface. The backing should be smooth, but not taut. For a big quilt, pin mark the center of each side of the backing before you lay it out, and place some masking tape at each of these pin marks, as shown.

If you are working on a table that is smaller than the quilt top, match the center of the backing with the center of the table, and anchor the backing in place with bulldog or binder clips. Anchor the backing first with clips at the centers of each side of the table, and then at the corners. Again, the backing should be smooth, but not taut.

2. Fold the batting into quarters and place it in one corner of the backing; then unfold the batting to cover the backing. For a large quilt, use the masking-tape markers or the clips to help you place the folded batting. Make sure the batting is smooth and without rumples.

3. Fold the quilt top into quarters, place it on top of one corner of the batting, and then unfold it to cover the batting. Again, for a big quilt, the center markings of masking tape or clips will help you place the quilt accurately.

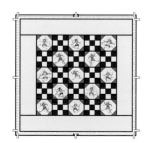

Basting

Basting holds your quilt layers together so they don't shift while you're doing the actual quilting. Basting for machine quilting is done with safety pins. Basting for hand quilting is done with thread.

Pin Basting

Pin basting is easiest to do in two steps. First, put all the safety pins in place, but leave them open. Second, go back and close all the pins. The reason for this two-step process is that the initial pinning does not disturb the layers, but closing the pins can.

1. Beginning in the center of the quilt, place safety pins across the width and along the center length of the quilt.

2. Pin one quarter of the quilt at a time, placing pins about 3" to 4" [8 to 10 cm] apart. You may place the pins at any angle that suits you, but try to keep them away from places you know you'll be quilting. For example, if you plan to quilt in the ditch around the patchwork shapes, place pins in the center of the shapes. If you plan to quilt a grid of straight or wiggly lines, place pins to avoid your planned quilting lines.

3. Close all the pins, using a small teaspoon to help you. Slide the bowl or handle of the spoon under the point of the pin, twist it slightly to lift the point, and close the pin.

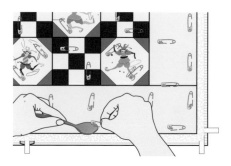

4. If you are working on a table that is smaller than the quilt top, pin the area of the top that's on the table; then undo the clips and gently slide the quilt over so that an unpinned side is flat on the table. Smooth out the layers, and continue pinning. Repeat as needed until the entire quilt is basted.

Thread Basting

Use a long needle, such as a darning needle, and a long length of light-colored thread (a dark thread could leave permanent marks on the quilt.) Tie a large knot at the end of the thread.

1. Beginning in the center of the quilt, take long running stitches to one side of the quilt. The stitches can be quite large. Starting back in the center, stitch to the opposite edge of the quilt. Repeat this process, stitching from the center to the top of the quilt and then from the center to the bottom. End each line of stitching with a couple of small backstitches, leaving a 1" [2.5 cm] tail of thread.

2. Beginning at the center each time, fill in each quadrant with a grid of stitching lines about 3" to 4" [8 to 10 cm] apart.

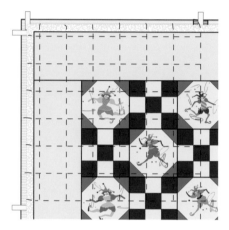

Baste each quadrant of the quilt.

3. If you are working on a table that is smaller than the quilt top, stitch all of the area that's on the table, but don't end off. Instead, leave the threads dangling where the quilt hangs over the table. Undo the clips and slide the quilt over so that an unstitched side is flat on the table. Smooth out the layers and use the dangling threads to finish the stitching. Repeat as needed until the whole quilt is basted.

Machine Quilting

Machine quilting is yet another magical aspect of today's quiltmaking. It is just as valid as hand quilting, and it's quicker to do. Quilting by machine is very practical and durable for quilts that will get a lot of use. In appearance, machine quilting makes a continuous line of stitches, unlike hand quilting, which makes a dashed line. There is no right or wrong method—the look is just different.

You will need your sewing machine, walking foot (for regular machine quilting), special or darning foot (for free-motion machine quilting), an extra table, soft cotton quilting gloves with rubber dots on the fingertips (optional), a chalk wheel or sliver of soap for marking designs, a long quilting ruler for marking straight lines or grid designs, and freezer paper for templates.

It is important that you set up your work area properly for machine quilting. Create a large flat space to the left of the machine so that the quilt will move smoothly through the machine with as little drag as possible.

A flatbed arrangement for your machine is ideal for machine quilting, which means that the machine is set down into a sewing table, with the bed of the machine at the same level as the table. If that's not possible, set up your machine so it has the maximum amount of flat area around the needle. Some machines have extension tables that slide onto the bed of the machine to give you a larger area for quilting. Completely clear your sewing table to your left.

Place a small table that is close to the same height as your sewing table on your left, to create an L-shaped workspace.

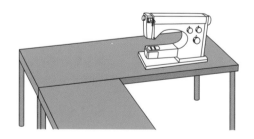

Setting Up for Quilting with a Walking Foot

1. Attach or engage the walking foot (consult your machine manual). This foot is very important because it helps the layers move together smoothly through the machine. Without a walking foot, the top layer may move ahead of the backing, which can cause puckers.

2. Set the machine stitch length to just above 2.5, or about 10 stitches per inch (a little longer than for piecing).

3. Choose a thread to blend in with the colors of your quilt. Try out thread colors by dangling loops of thread on top of the quilt to see which suits best. Medium-value colors often work well. Sometimes you may need to use different colors for different parts of the quilt.

4. If required, mark quilting lines on your layered and basted quilt with a chalk wheel or sliver of soap. Mark only one or two lines at a time, just before stitching, as these lines rub off easily as the quilt gets handled.

5. A small quilt can be scrunched up to fit under the arm of the machine, but larger quilts need to be rolled up. Roll up the quilt from the edges, leaving a space in the center where you will begin to quilt.

6. Move the rolled-up quilt to the machine. Position the right-hand roll so that it will move through the space under the arm of the machine.

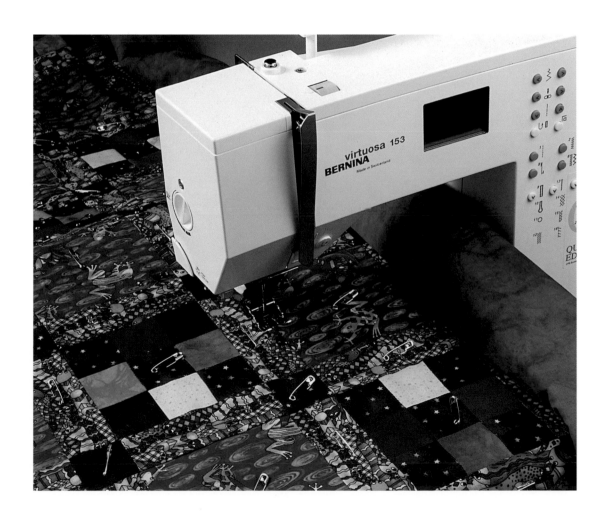

Machine Quilting Basics

Here are some general tips for basic machine quilting:

- To start and stop lines of quilting, set the stitch length to almost 0 and take a few tiny stitches to lock the thread. Reset the stitch length to continue quilting. Alternatively, you can stitch forward and then backstitch two stitches to secure the threads.

- As you quilt, smooth the quilt in front of the needle by using your hands on either side of the needle to put gentle pressure sideways on the quilt. If you feel the top layer tending to bunch up and move ahead of the other layers, exert more sideways pressure with your hands.

- Concentrate on keeping the area where you are stitching nice and flat. The rest of the quilt will be rolled or scrunched up, with the safety pins holding the layers firmly in place, ready for you to smooth out a space when you come to it. Don't let any of the quilt drop over the edge of the table, as it will drag, and your stitches won't form evenly.

- When you stop for any reason, always stop with the needle in the down position so that when you resume stitching, the line will continue smoothly. If the needle is up, the quilt may move slightly, and the stitching line can become a little jagged.

- Pivot by stopping the machine with the needle down. Then lift the presser foot, turn the quilt (unrolling and rerolling it as necessary), lower

the presser foot, and continue stitching in the new direction.

- Always quilt the longest or main lines first, such as along the lines between the blocks or sashing. Then fill in with the shorter lines.

- When the quilt is finished, either snip the ends of the secured threads or sew in the thread ends by hand.

Designs for Quilting with a Walking Foot

You can achieve a number of different looks by machine quilting with the walking foot.

Quilting in the ditch. This technique is also called "outline quilting." With this type of quilting, you stitch along a seam line, stitching in the little ditch created along the side of the seam that does not have the seam allowances beneath it. You may have to switch sides from one side of a seam line to the other at times, depending on which way the seam allowances have been pressed. Appliqué shapes can be outlined by stitching along the background just outside the shape, which will have the effect of puffing up the shape.

Straight-line quilting. Mark straight lines with chalk or a sliver of soap and your long quilting ruler. Mark lines just before sewing, as both chalk and soap can rub off easily when the quilt is handled. Simple diagonal grids of squares work well on many quilts, especially quilts that are made from lots of squares, such as Four Patch and Nine Patch quilts.

Wavy-line quilting. Wavy or wiggly lines are easy to quilt. The lines can be vertical, horizontal, or diagonal, and when crossed, give a jigsaw look. The lines do not need to be marked—you can use the position of the safety pins as a guide. (When pinning, plan ahead to place the pins so that they create channels for you to sew between.)

Echo quilting. This method results in quilt lines a fixed distance around or inside a shape. You

can use the width of your walking foot as a guide or mark lines with chalk or soap.

Combinations. You can use a mixture of these styles for different areas of the quilt. For example, you may want to outline quilt appliqué or pieced shapes, echo quilt lines on the background, and quilt straight lines in the borders. Areas of free-motion machine quilting (see the following section) also combine well with lines of machine quilting done with a walking foot.

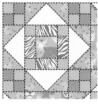
Quilting in the Ditch

Straight-Line Quilting

Wavy-Line Quilting

Echo Quilting

Free-Motion Machine Quilting

To understand **free-motion machine quilting**, imagine that you have a pencil fixed in a clamp with its point on a piece of paper on the table beneath it. You draw by moving the paper under the pencil instead of the other way around. Although you can start and stop, it's best if the line is continuous—like doodling without lifting the pencil. Therefore you need to choose or create patterns that do not require repeated starting and stopping.

Instead of the pencil, you will be using your machine needle to make a continuous quilting line. The skill lies in moving the quilt sandwich smoothly under the machine needle as it continues to make stitches. Free-motion machine quilting is like learning to drive—at first it will seem that there is a lot to remember at once, but as you practice, it will become easier. When you get going, you will find free-motion machine quilting a lot of fun and a quick way to finish your quilts.

Free-motion machine quilting is done as its name indicates—freely. It is difficult to follow a line in the way you do when using a walking foot. For free-motion quilting, many simple patterns are not marked before stitching. However, it is possible to mark a few lines to give you a general direction in which to take your stitching. Mark these lines with a chalk wheel or sliver of soap. Simple shapes, such as hearts, can be cut from freezer paper and ironed on, to give a temporary guide.

Setting Up for Free-Motion Quilting

1. Set up space around the machine as for basic machine quilting, described previously. Remove or disengage the walking foot and attach the darning foot or special-purpose free-motion machine quilting foot. This foot will help hold the quilt sandwich in place while you are stitching, yet its spring action lets you move the quilt freely beneath the needle.

2. Drop the feed dogs (consult your machine instructions for this). This stops the machine from moving the fabric from front to back as it normally does. Instead, you'll be moving the quilt with your hands.

3. Choose a quilting thread to achieve the effect you want. It can match one of the fabrics, blend in with all the fabrics, or contrast with the fabrics.

4. Adjust the tension of the machine for free-motion machine quilting. See "Machine Tension for Free-Motion Quilting" at right.

MACHINE TENSION FOR FREE-MOTION QUILTING

To find the correct tension for free-motion quilting, make a small sample. Sandwich together a short strip of batting between two strips of scrap fabric. Mark the strip into six sections and label them 2 through 7. Set the tension on 2 (or the loose setting on your machine), and quilt some curves and loops across section 2, ending at the division line. Stop quilting and turn the tension to 3 (a little tighter); then continue quilting across section 3 to the next line.

Continue sewing in this manner across the sample, changing the tension in each division. Take the sample from the machine and check the stitching on both sides. It should be even front and back. If there are loops on the back, the tension is too loose, or if the bobbin thread is coming through to the top, the tension is too tight. Note the number where the tension is right, and use this setting. This procedure may need to be redone if you change kinds of thread, batting, or fabric.

Loops on Back

Bumps on Top

5. Arrange the quilt so that the area you are about to quilt is flat around the needle and the surrounding area is lightly scrunched up around the center space—like a valley with hills in a semicircle around it. The looseness in the scrunching will give you a bit of play when moving the quilt. For a large quilt, roll up the remainder of the quilt to fit under the arm of the machine.

6. Place your hands flat on the quilt so that they encircle each side of the needle. That way you can easily move the quilt with your hands. If you cannot grip the fabric sufficiently, try cotton gloves with rubber tips on the fingers.

The Quilting Process

1. Begin by making about five tiny stitches that are so small they are almost on top of each other.

2. Run the machine at a steady pace while smoothly moving the quilt with your hands, guiding the quilt to follow the pattern you are stitching. If the stitches are very small, you are stitching too fast and you need to slow down the machine speed while moving your hands as before. If the stitches are too long, you need to make the machine stitch more quickly. Find the combination of machine speed and quilt movement that is most comfortable for you.

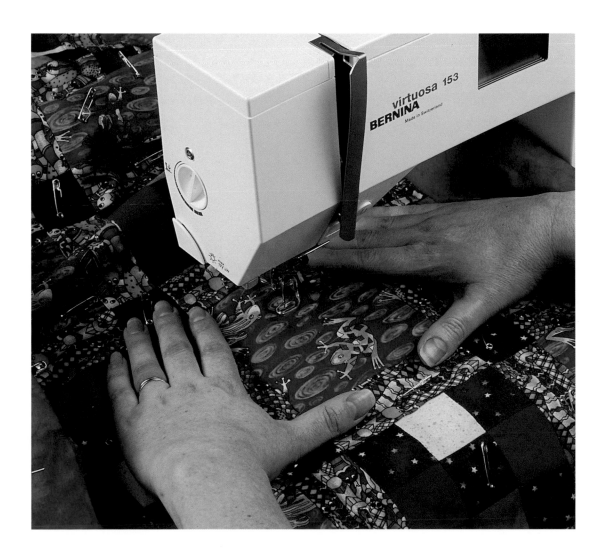

3. As you sew, concentrate only on the space around the needle. Make sure that all of the quilt is on top of your work surface and not drooping over the edges, which could cause it to drag and make uneven stitches.

4. When filling spaces with random quilting, think ahead as you go. You don't want to box yourself into a corner.

5. Remove safety pins as you go if they are in the way.

6. Finish by taking five tiny stitches. Snip off all thread ends or bury them in the quilt layers by threading them on a needle and sewing them in by hand.

LEARN TO RELAX

The most important part of free-motion machine quilting is the tension—yours, not the machine's! If you are tense, the quilting will not go so smoothly. Try the following hints to keep your quilting relaxed.

- Turn on music that you like. Try some lilting melodies.

- Use good posture, sitting with your back straight and your hands relaxed and flat.

- Before you begin, tense your shoulders tightly, and then let them totally relax.

- Remember to breathe normally. If you are tense you may find you are holding your breath.

- Loosen up on a practice piece.

- Think about free-motion machine quilting as just doodling or scribbling.

- Take frequent short breaks to stretch your arms, back, and legs.

Designs for Free-Motion Quilting

Meandering or stippling. A line that meanders around in small curves is the most common free-motion design. Tighter curves are called stippling. Try small curves at first, as larger curves take more practice. Note that the closer the stitching lines, the more the quilt will be flattened; close stippling may make a quilt feel quite stiff. Meander quilting is good filler for background areas, making areas that are less heavily quilted stand out. A large meander can work well over a whole quilt, especially where the prints are busy.

Loops. Stitching loops is done like meandering, except that in this design you deliberately cross the lines to make loops.

Waves. Waves are another design that you can use to fill in large areas or use as an allover design for a quilt top. Make waves going in all directions.

Spirals. To make spirals, start a large circle and continue spiraling inward; then reverse and stitch your way back out. Remember to leave yourself space to get back out again!

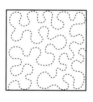

Meander

Loops

Waves

Spirals

FREE-MOTION QUILTING EXERCISE

Try these exercises to get a feel for the motion. Then you'll be ready to tackle your quilt.

You will need: paper, pencil, two 20" [50 cm] squares of scrap fabrics and one of batting, safety pins, darning foot, and machine quilting thread.

1. Using a pencil and paper, doodle the patterns on page 86 without lifting your pencil from the paper as you draw. This will keep the line continuous. Try filling the space into a corner so that you practice getting in and out of a defined space.

2. Layer the squares of fabric with batting in between. Pin the layers together with safety pins. Practice meandering first, to get the feel of the movement and the speed of the stitching. Then try other designs.

3. Continue practicing until you are confident in moving the fabric and able to make relatively even stitches.

Hand Quilting

Hand quilting gives a beautiful, traditional finish to a quilt and is always highly valued. While it can take a considerable amount of time to do, many quilters enjoy the process of hand quilting. Hand quilting is portable, so you can join your family while they're watching television, or even take your quilting on a trip.

You will need hand-quilting thread, a Between needle (size 8 is good for beginners), quilting hoop, two thimbles (or one thimble and a finger protector), embroidery scissors, pencil, and quilting design or stencil. It is important to choose a batting that is recommended for hand quilting.

Marking Quilting Designs

For hand quilting, the designs generally need to be marked on the quilt before you layer the quilt top, batting, and backing. Mark designs using a pencil and mark the lines lightly—but not so lightly that you cannot see them. On dark fabrics, use a silver pencil. Use your long ruler as a guide for drawing lines and grids. For shapes, you can cut designs out of cardboard or plastic and then draw around them. On light fabrics, trace designs by taping the design to the table, placing the quilt top over the design, and copying it carefully. On dark fabrics, tape the design and the fabric to a window. Plastic quilting stencils have designs punched into them so that you can place the stencil on top of the quilt top and draw the design through the punched lines. This makes stencils a good choice for dark or light fabrics.

Some quilting does not require prior marking, such as quilting in the ditch of the seams. Chalk or soap slivers make temporary lines that can be drawn on the quilt after it has been layered and basted, just before you begin to stitch. You can also place masking tape where you need a straight line and stitch alongside it. (Don't leave masking tape on the quilt while you are not actually quilting; it may leave a sticky residue if left in place too long.)

Preparing to Quilt

1. Mark any quilting lines or motifs, and then layer and thread baste your quilt as described on page 78–80.

2. Always begin quilting in the center of the quilt. Place the prepared quilt on top of the inner ring of the quilting hoop. Place the outer ring on top of the quilt and bring it down over the inner ring. Tighten the screws of the outer ring so that the quilt is held firmly, but not too tightly. The quilt should fit softly across the

hoop; you need some flexibility to get the needle in and out of the fabric.

3. Set yourself up comfortably in a chair with your quilting equipment handy. The arms of a chair can help support the hoop as you work.

HAND QUILTING EXERCISE

The rocking motion of hand quilting may seem a little awkward at first, but you'll soon master it after a little bit of practice.

You will need: two squares of cream fabric and one square of batting, all 28" [70 cm] square; quilting thread and hand quilting equipment.

1. Trace the quilting design from page 108 onto one square of cream fabric. Add some framing lines around the design if you wish.

2. Layer the marked cream fabric with batting and backing, and thread baste the layers together.

3. Put the prepared piece in your quilting hoop and practice quilting.

The Quilting Action

There is no one right way to hand quilt; different people prefer different methods and like to use slightly different equipment. The important thing to keep in mind is that the stitches must go through all three layers of the quilt. That's the top priority. Next, aim to make your stitches even. After you've mastered that, it just takes practice so that your stitches become neat and small.

Hand quilting involves using both hands. The quilt hoop holds the layers in place, leaving your hands free to stitch. Your dominant hand goes on top of the quilt, and it will hold the needle and make the stitches. Your other hand goes beneath the quilt, where the index finger will guide the stitches, ensuring that the stitches go through the three layers. Pushing the needle through the layers of the quilt requires some force, so wear a thimble on the middle finger of the hand holding the needle. The index finger of your hand beneath the quilt also needs protection from the tip of the needle. This can be another metal thimble, or some other form of protection, such as a leather dot (with adhesive to stick it in place), a small circle of metal (also with adhesive), a leather thimble with a metal tip, or a plastic protector. The choice here is personal, and you'll most likely be able to find any of these gadgets at your local quilt shop.

1. Cut a piece of quilting thread about as long as your forearm. Thread the Between needle and tie a knot at the thread end (see page 58).

2. Place a thimble on the middle finger of the hand holding the needle. Put a thimble or other protector on the index finger of your other hand.

3. Begin by burying the knot in the batting, either by coming through from underneath the quilt and pulling the knot gently into the batting (too strong a pull and it will come right through the quilt) or by taking a stitch about ½" [1 cm] long on the top of the quilt and pulling the knot into the batting. Either way, make your needle come out exactly on the quilting line where you want to begin.

4. Position your sewing hand on top of the quilt and the other hand beneath it. Grasp the needle between your thumb and index finger, with either the side or the top of the thimble behind the needle (whichever is more comfortable for you), ready to push the needle forward.

5. Push the needle down through the layers of the quilt. At the same time, use the index finger of the hand beneath the quilt to feel where the needle is coming through. Rock the needle back upward so that it takes a small stitch, using your index finger below to help guide it.

6. Repeat this rocking action—pushing the needle down through the layers and then rocking it back upward and out again, all the while feeling and guiding with the finger of the bottom hand—to make several small stitches on the needle at one time. Then pull the needle through the layers so that the thread makes

the stitches. Use the thimble to push the needle from behind as you pull on the front end of the needle.

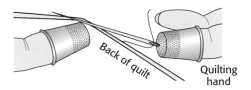

7. Continue stitching in this manner along your marked lines.

8. When you come to a bulky area where there are layers of seam allowance, take only one stitch at a time using the stab stitch. Stitch straight down through all layers and pull the needle out of the fabric from beneath the quilt. Then sew straight up in a separate motion.

9. To end the stitching, take one small stab stitch down and then bring the needle back up through the layers about halfway along the stitch you just took (a half backstitch). Stick the needle back into the same hole as the last stitch, but don't go through all the layers. Instead, just stitch into the batting for about 1" [2.5 cm]. Bring the needle back up to the top of the quilt and snip off the thread.

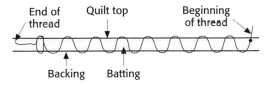

Finishing Your Quilt

The last phase in making your quilt is binding the edges.

You may also add a sleeve if you want to hang the quilt.

We strongly recommend that you add a label to the back of your quilt. Don't leave your great-grandchildren wondering who made it!

Binding

Quilt **binding** is made of strips of fabric that wrap around and finish the edges of the quilt, encasing the raw edges and the batting. While there are various methods for applying binding, we like to use four separate strips, one for each side of the quilt. That way you can cut binding strips to the correct length based on the measurement of your quilt center, just as you did for borders. As a result, the binding will fit nicely, the quilt edges will not be wavy, and the quilt will lie flat and square.

1. Using your long ruler and rotary cutter, trim the excess batting and backing fabric from all edges of the quilt, leaving ¼" [6 mm] of batting and backing outside the raw edge of the quilt top. This extra bit of batting will fill out the binding.

2. Cut binding strips 2½" [7 cm] wide and about 2" [5 cm] longer than the sides of the quilt they are to bind.

3. If needed, join strips to make them long enough to fit your quilt edges. (See "Joining Binding Strips" on the facing page.)

4. Fold the binding strips in half lengthwise with wrong sides together and press.

5. Lay the quilt out flat in a clear space. Pin mark the centers of the four sides of the quilt.

6. Lay the prepared side binding strips over the center length of the quilt. Pin mark the strips at each end so the pins are parallel to the edges of the quilt top. Pin mark the center of each binding strip. Pin the strips to the sides of the quilt, matching the raw edges of the binding strips to the edge of the quilt top. Match the pin marks to the edges of the quilt and the center of the quilt sides, making sure the strips are straight. Pin the strips to the quilt as you did for borders (see pages 72–73) by pinning in the center portion between the pins until there are pins along the entire edge about 2" to 3" [5 cm to 8 cm] apart. You may have to stretch gently or ease the binding to fit the quilt.

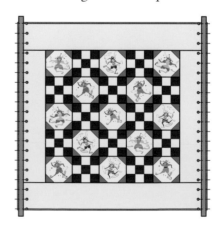

7. Using a walking foot, sew the binding in place with a ¼" [7.5 mm] seam allowance. (You may have to do a little practice beforehand to ensure the ¼" [7.5 mm] seam, as the walking foot may obscure your seam-guide marking.) If necessary, gently pull the binding in the direction of the stitching as you sew, stretching it a little to take up any fullness in the quilt.

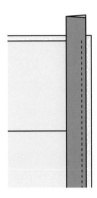

8. Trim the ends of the binding even with the edges of the quilt. Fold the binding over to the back of the quilt and pin it in place. The edge of the binding should just cover the stitching.

Fold to back and pin.

JOINING BINDING STRIPS

You can join binding strips either on the diagonal or with a crosswise seam. Either way, press the seam allowances open to reduce bulk when the binding strips get folded in half. When the binding is finished, the diagonal seam will be spread apart on the front and back of the quilt, further reducing bulk and keeping the binding smooth. If your binding fabric is striped, use the straight seam so that you can match the stripes easily.

Diagonal seam. To join binding strips on the diagonal, place the two strips right sides together at a right angle to one another. Make the ends of the strips extend by about ¼" [7.5 mm], as shown. Pin the strips together, and then mark a line on the diagonal from corner to corner as shown. Sew along the line, trim away the excess fabric leaving a ¼" [7.5 mm] seam allowance, and press the seam allowance open. Trim away the ears.

Crosswise seam. To join binding strips with a crosswise seam, first square up the ends of the strips. Align the ends of the strips with fabric right sides together. Sew a ¼" [7.5 mm] seam. Press the seam allowance open.

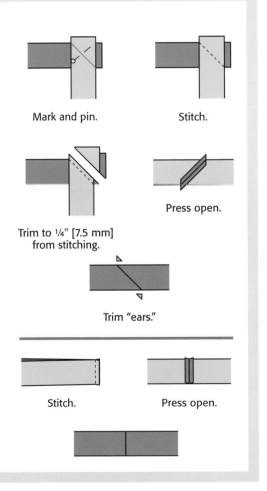

Mark and pin.

Stitch.

Trim to ¼" [7.5 mm] from stitching.

Press open.

Trim "ears."

Stitch.

Press open.

9. Lay the remaining two binding strips across the horizontal center of the quilt and pin mark them at the edges where the side bindings are joined to the quilt. Pin mark the centers of the binding strips; then pin and sew the strips to the top and bottom of the quilt as you did for the side bindings. Fold the binding to the back of the quilt and pin.

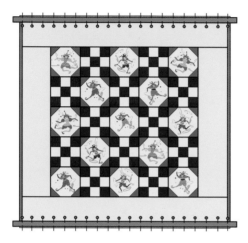

10. Hand stitch the binding to the back of the quilt using thread that matches the binding. Make corners neat and square as follows. To reduce bulk, trim each corner by making a diagonal cut ⅛" [5 mm] above the stitching that holds the binding. Trim the binding so that it extends about ⅜" [1 cm] from the edge of the quilt. First, firmly fold the end around to the back so that the fold is parallel to the side edge of the quilt. Then fold the binding over and stitch in place.

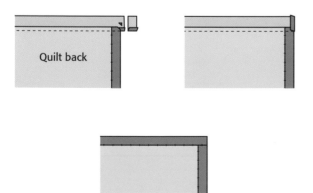

Hanging Sleeves

A **hanging sleeve** is a tube of fabric sewn to the top back of a quilt so that a rod can be inserted to hang the quilt on a wall or in an exhibition. Below are instructions for making a 4" finished-width sleeve.

1. From backing fabric, cut a strip 8½" [21.5 cm] wide. If the quilt is large, cut and join two strips.

2. Square up one end of the strip and press a ⅜" [1 cm] hem in the end. Stitch the hem in place.

3. Lay out the quilt in a clear space and lay the prepared strip across the top of the quilt with the hemmed end just inside the side binding. Pin mark the strip at the other end, a little in from the binding on the other side. Trim the strip ¾" [2 cm] beyond the pin mark, and then press and sew a ⅜" [1 cm] hem on this end.

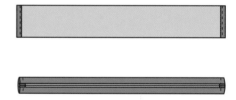

4. Fold the strip in half lengthwise with wrong sides together, and stitch along the length using a ¼" [7.5 mm] seam allowance. Press so that the seam is open and at the center of the sleeve. Pin the sleeve in place just below the binding with the seam side against the quilt, and hand stitch in place. Make sure your stitches do not go through to the front of the quilt.

Quilt Labels

A label on the back of the quilt identifies the maker's name, the name of the quilt, and any other information desired, such as the date made, quilt size, kind of batting used (useful information for later laundering), or the maker's address. It also can be a place to add a special message, such as birthday greetings or wedding congratulations. A label makes a quilt more special and ensures that the quilt, and all your work, will not become anonymous.

To make a label, you can either write on a square or rectangle of fabric in permanent ink, or embroider the label by hand or machine. Press a seam allowance around the shape, and then hand stitch in place.

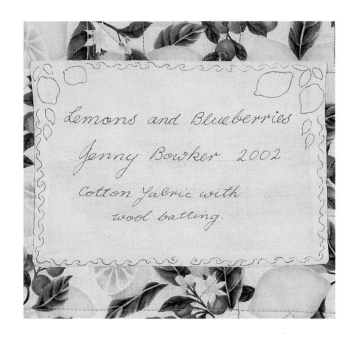

Designing a Quilt

Some people find the word "designing" scary. But there's nothing

to be afraid of! Designing is simply playing with the possibilities.

It is exploring the question, "What happens if I ... ?"

When you design, you are the magician who can wave your wand

and make wonderful things happen.

The arrangement of the blocks and elements of the quilt is called the **quilt set** or **setting**. There are lots of simple things that you can do to arrange, rearrange and, in short, play with blocks, to determine your final quilt setting. We will use the Evening Star block as an example. Look carefully at each of the following designs, noticing how changes are made by the way the block is set.

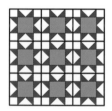
Repeating Blocks

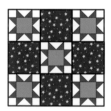
Alternating with Plain Blocks

Alternating with Simply-Pieced Blocks

Alternating with a Secondary Block

Alternating Value Placement

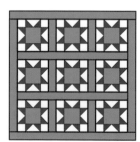
Adding Sashing Strips

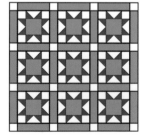
Adding Sashing Strips with Cornerstones

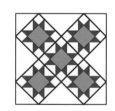
Turning Blocks on Point

Turning Blocks on Point and Using Alternate Plain Blocks

Surrounding Blocks

You can change the look of blocks by surrounding them with contrasting fabric so that they appear framed, or background fabric so that they appear to float.

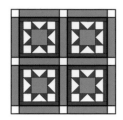
Framing the Block

Floating the Block

Blocks That Form Secondary Designs

Blocks whose pieces form a diagonal design will create different effects when they are repeated. The Double X block shown here is a good example.

Repeating a Block with a Diagonal

Rotating Alternate Blocks

Designing with Log Cabin Blocks

Because they are half light and half dark, working with traditional Log Cabin blocks is essentially like working with half-square triangle units. Each block can be rotated into four different positions, just like a half-square triangle unit. So, Log Cabin blocks, as well as any other blocks that have the effect of forming triangles, can be arranged to make many patterns.

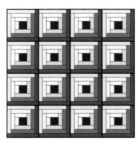

Straight Furrows

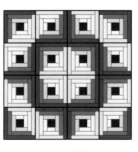
Barn Raising

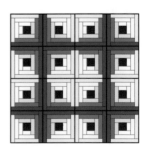
Sunshine and Shadow

PRETTY PANSIES by Margaret Rolfe

This is an ideal first quilt to make because it is a simple design and a manageable size. You will practice the basic skills of accurate cutting and sewing and learn to assemble a quilt. It makes a delightful lap or child's quilt, depending upon your fabric choices.

Size of quilt top: 39½" x 47½" [99 cm x 119 cm]
Finished block size: 4" [10 cm]

Four Patch Block

Materials

Amounts are based on 42" [106 cm]-wide fabric.

Choose your fabrics by first selecting a feature fabric; then look for the other fabrics to coordinate with it. Choose a light background for the alternate blocks and two contrasting prints for the Four Patch blocks, one a lighter value than the other. The binding can be any one of the fabrics used in the quilt, in which case you'll add the quantities together, or you can choose a new fabric for the binding.

- ¾ yard [70 cm] of feature fabric for border

- ⅝ yard [50 cm] of light print for background squares

- ⅓ yard [30 cm] of first contrast print for Four Patch blocks

- ⅓ yard [30 cm] of second contrast print for Four Patch blocks

- 1½ yards [1.3 m] of print for backing

- ½ yard [40 cm] of print for binding

- 43" x 51" [109 cm x 129 cm] piece of batting

Cutting

Review "Preparing Fabric for Cutting," page 37, and "Rotary Cutting," page 35. Cut across the width of the fabric.

From the first contrast print, cut:
- 4 strips, 2½" [6.5 cm] wide

From the second contrast print, cut:
- 4 strips, 2½" [6.5 cm] wide

From the fabric for background squares, cut:
- 4 strips, 4½" [11.5 cm] wide; crosscut into 32 squares, 4½" x 4½" [11.5 cm x 11.5 cm]

From the feature fabric for border, cut:
- 4 strips, 6" [15 cm] wide

From the fabric for binding, cut:
- 5 strips, 2½" [7 cm] wide

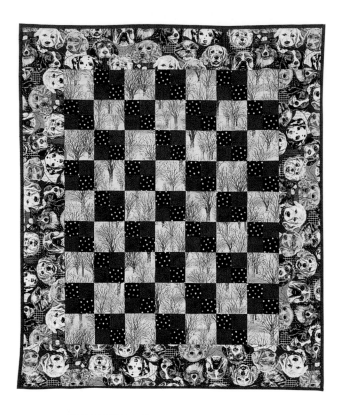

WALKIES TIME by Margaret Rolfe

TEDDY BEAR PLAYTIME by Margaret Rolfe

NAP TIME by Margaret Rolfe

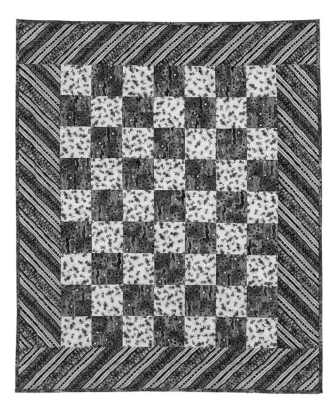

MARY'S CHOICE by Margaret Rolfe

Making the Four Patch Blocks

Review "Strip Piecing," page 49.

1. Sew together a strip of each of the contrast prints. Press the seam toward the darker fabric. Repeat with the remaining strips to make four sets of strips.

Make 4 strip sets.

2. Square up the end of each strip set, and crosscut the strip sets into 62 segments, 2½" [6.5 cm] wide.

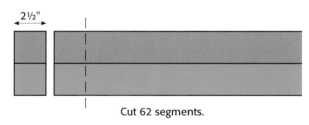

2½"

Cut 62 segments.

3. Join the segments to make 31 Four Patch blocks.

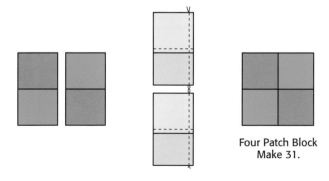

Four Patch Block
Make 31.

SAME COLOR ON TOP

Be careful to join the pieces with the same patch at the top each time; otherwise some of your Four Patch blocks may have a diagonal going in the opposite direction.

Assembling the Quilt

Review "Quilt-Top Assembly," page 68.

1. Join the background squares and Four Patch blocks into rows, as shown. Press the seams in opposite directions from row to row. Make nine rows, five beginning with a background square and four beginning with a Four Patch.

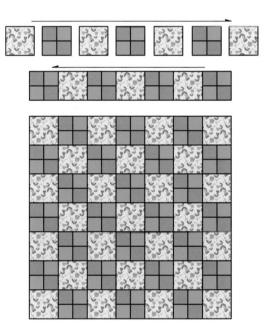

2. Sew the rows together to make the quilt center and press.

Adding the Borders

1. Using two of the border strips, square up one end of each strip. Measure the strips to fit the length of the quilt, referring to "Butted Corners" on page 73. Cut the strips to this length. Pin and sew the border strips to the quilt sides. Press the seam allowances toward the borders.

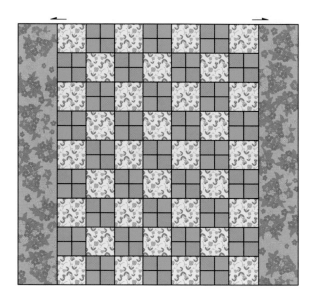

2. Square up one end of each of the two remaining border strips. Measure the strips to fit the width of the quilt, again referring to "Adding Borders." Cut the strips to this length. Pin and sew them to the top and bottom of the quilt. Press the seam allowances toward the borders.

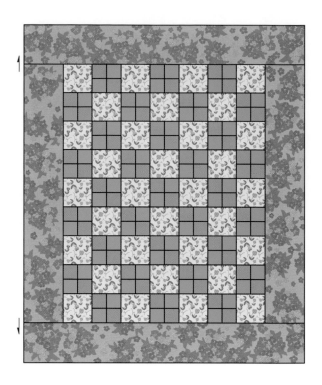

Quilting

1. Layer the backing, batting, and quilt top, referring to "Layering" on page 78.

2. Baste the layers together, referring to "Pin Basting" on page 79 if you'll be machine quilting or "Thread Basting" on page 79 if you'll be hand quilting.

3. Quilt as desired. You can use grids of straight lines either on the square or diagonal, or grids of wiggly lines, as shown in the quilt samples. Quilt straight or wiggly lines into the borders.

Finishing

Review "Binding" on page 90.

1. Cut one of the 2½" [7 cm]-wide binding strips in half. Join a half strip to two of the remaining strips to make two longer strips.

2. Attach the binding to your quilt.

Four Patch Variations

You can customize the quilt to suit a baby or toddler, a boy or girl, a man or woman,

a dog or cat lover—or anyone—simply based on your choice of feature fabric for the border.

MYTHS AND LEGENDS by Margaret Rolfe

FLOWER POWER by Margaret Rolfe

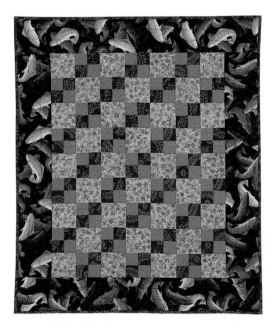

GONE FISHIN' by Margaret Rolfe

PINK AND BLUE BOUQUET by Margaret Rolfe

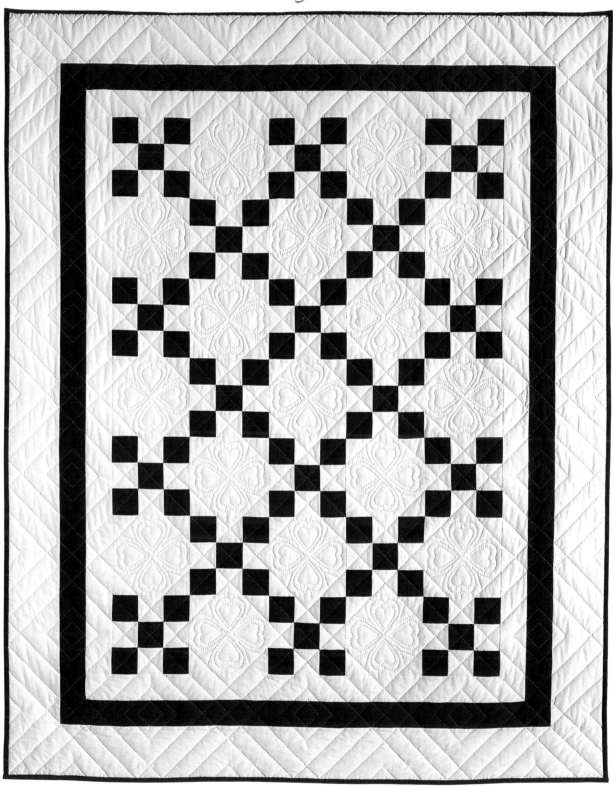

HEART TO HEART by Margaret Rolfe

A classic Nine Patch, this quilt can be made from just two fabrics, yet the look can be quite different depending on whether prints or solids are used. You will be amazed at how quickly the Nine Patch blocks can be made by strip piecing. This project is excellent for practicing your hand quilting if you use solid fabrics for the alternate blocks. If you opt for a print fabric, you might want to machine quilt since fine hand quilting won't show as well on a multicolor print.

Size of quilt top: 58" x 73" [139.5 cm x 175.5 cm]
Finished block size: 7½" [18 cm]

Nine Patch Block

Materials

Amounts are based on 42" [106 cm]-wide fabric.

- 3½ yards [3 m] of print or solid background fabric for Nine Patch blocks, alternate blocks, and first and third borders

- 1¾ yards [1.6 m] of print or solid contrast fabric for Nine Patch blocks, second border, and binding

- 3½ yards [3.1 m] of backing fabric

- 62" x 77" [148 cm x 184 cm] piece of batting

Cutting

Cut across the width of the fabric, unless otherwise specified.

From the contrast fabric, cut:
- 14 strips, 3" [7.5 cm] wide
- 7 strips, 2½" [7 cm] wide

From the background fabric, cut:
- 7 strips, 3" [7.5 cm] wide
- 4 strips, 8" [19.5 cm] wide; crosscut into 17 squares, 8" x 8" [19.5 cm x 19.5 cm]

From the remaining background fabric, cut on the lengthwise grain, referring to "Cutting Lengthwise Strips" on page 43:
- 4 strips, 5½" [13.5 cm] wide x length of fabric
- 4 strips, 3" [7.5 cm] wide x length of fabric

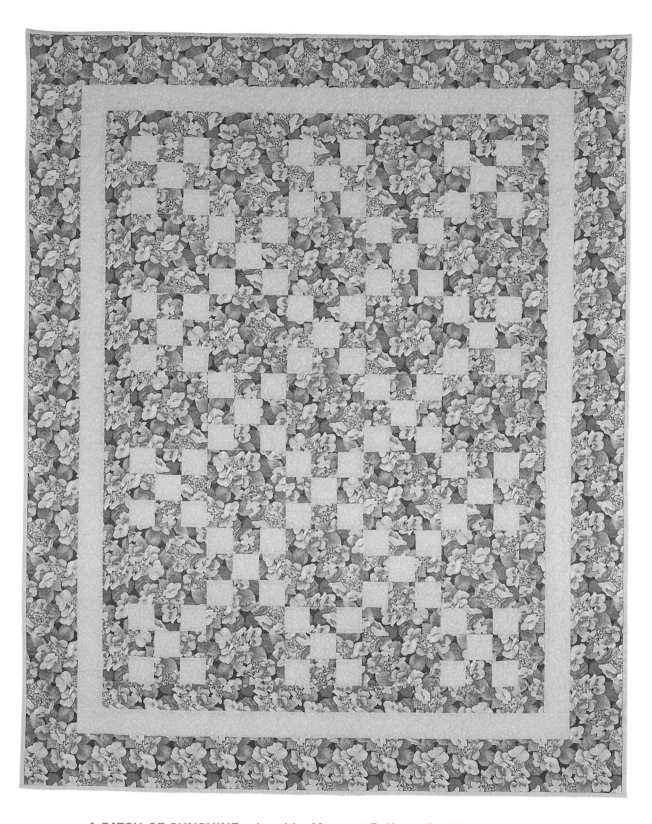

A PATCH OF SUNSHINE, pieced by Margaret Rolfe, quilted by Jenny Bowker

Making the Nine Patch Blocks

Review "Strip Piecing Nine Patch Blocks," page 50. To make the blocks, use only the background strips that you cut across the width of the fabric. The strips cut lengthwise will be used later for the borders.

1. Use 3" [7.5 cm]-wide strips of contrast fabric and background fabric to make three strip sets, each with a contrast fabric strip on the outside and a background strip in the center, as shown. Press the seam allowances toward the contrast fabric.

Make 3 strip sets.

2. Crosscut the sets into 36 segments, 3" [7.5 cm] wide.

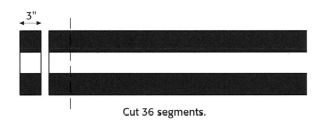

Cut 36 segments.

3. Use 3" [7.5 cm]-wide strips of background fabric and contrast fabric to make two strip sets, each with background fabric on the outside and contrast fabric in the center, as shown. Press the seam allowances toward the contrast fabric.

Make 2 strip sets.

4. Crosscut the sets into 18 segments, 3" [7.5 cm] wide.

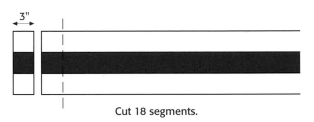

Cut 18 segments.

5. Join the two different types of segments to make 18 Nine Patch blocks.

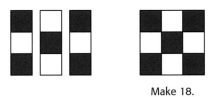

Make 18.

Assembling the Quilt

Review "Quilt-Top Assembly," page 68.

1. Lay out the Nine Patch blocks and squares of background fabric in rows as shown.

2. Join the blocks into rows, pressing the seam allowances toward the background squares.

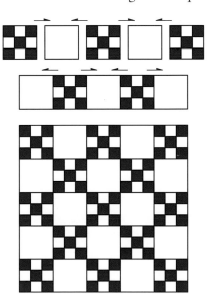

3. Sew the rows together to make the quilt center.

Adding the Borders

1. Using two of the 3" [7.5 cm]-wide background fabric strips cut on the lengthwise grain, square up one end of each strip. Measure the strips to fit the length of the quilt, referring to "Butted Corners" on page 73. Cut the strips to this length. Pin and sew the borders to the quilt sides. Press the seam allowances toward the borders.

2. Square up one end of each of the two remaining 3" [7.5 cm]-wide strips of background fabric cut on the lengthwise grain. Measure the strips to fit the width of the quilt, again referring to "Butted Corners." Cut the strips to this length. Pin and sew them to the top and bottom of the quilt. Press the seam allowances toward the borders.

3. Cut two of the 3" [7.5 cm]-wide contrast fabric strips in half to make four half strips. Join each of these half strips to one end of a remaining 3" [7.5 cm]-wide strip to make four long border strips.

4. Using these strips of contrast fabric, add the second border in the same manner as for the first border, described in steps 1 and 2 above.

5. Using the four 5½" [13.5 cm]-wide background fabric strips, add the third border, following steps 1 and 2 above.

Quilting

1. Cut the backing fabric in half crosswise and join the two halves side by side; your backing will have a horizontal seam.

2. If you plan to hand quilt, mark the quilting design onto the quilt top. See page 108 for suggested designs. Layer the backing, batting, and quilt top, referring to "Layering" on page 78. Trim away the excess backing fabric.

3. Baste the layers together, referring to "Pin Basting" on page 79 if you'll be machine quilting or "Thread Basting" on page 79 if you'll be hand quilting.

4. Quilt as desired. One suggestion is to hand quilt motifs (see designs on page 108) onto background blocks and a grid of diagonal lines and squares onto the Nine Patch blocks and borders, following the corners of Nine Patch blocks as was done in "Heart to Heart." Or, you might wish to free-motion machine quilt a large meander design all over the quilt as in "A Patch of Sunshine."

Finishing

Review "Binding" on page 90.

1. Cut one of the 2½" [7 cm]-wide binding strips in half. Join a half strip to two of the remaining strips to make two longer strips. Sew the remaining four strips together into two pairs.

2. Attach the binding to your quilt.

Nine Patch Variation

With black as the background and rich solid colors used for contrast, the quilt has an Amish feel. You can make this variation by using shorter strips to make your strip sets so that you can vary the colors of the individual blocks.

ALMOST AMISH by Jenny Bowker

Suggested Quilting Plan

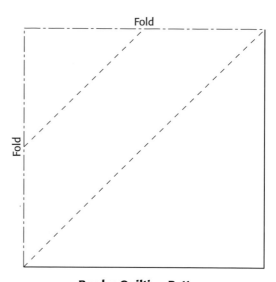

Border Quilting Pattern
Cut out a 5" (15 cm) square of tracing paper and fold it into quarters. Trace the design onto one quarter; then complete the design for the remaining three quarters.

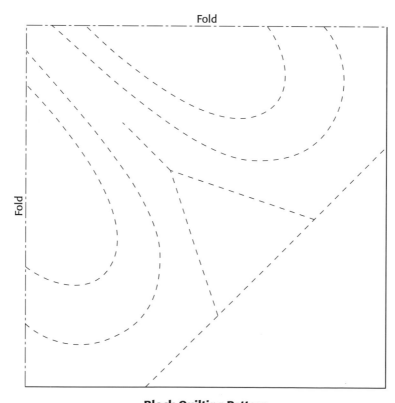

Block Quilting Pattern
Cut out a 7½" (20 cm) square of tracing paper and fold it into quarters. Trace the design onto one quarter; then complete design for the remaining three quarters.

LEMONS AND BLUEBERRIES by Jenny Bowker

It is fun to make a sampler quilt because you can try out different blocks as you learn new skills. We have designed this quilt to teach you all the piecing skills we have described in this book—cutting and sewing the various shapes, as well as using different techniques, such as flying-geese units and the stitch-and-fold-corner technique that we used in the sashing. Choose three coordinating fabrics for this quilt: a light value, a medium value, and a dark value. The light value becomes the background, and the other fabrics form the patchwork patterns. See the photograph on page 119 for an entirely different color scheme.

Size of quilt top: 54½" x 54½" [139.5 cm x 139.5 cm]
Finished block size: 9" [24 cm]

Materials

Amounts are based on 42" [106 cm]-wide fabric.

- 2¼ yards [2 m] of dark-value print
- 1½ yards [1.4 m] of light-value print
- 1¼ yards [1.2 m] of medium-value print
- 3½ yards [3.1 m] of backing fabric
- 58" x 58" [148 cm x 148 cm] piece of batting

Cutting Strips for the Blocks

Cut across the width of the fabric. As some of the strips and squares are similar in size, make size labels and pin them to the strips and squares for easy reference later. Review "Preparing Fabric for Cutting" on page 37, "Cutting Strips" on page 40, and "Crosscutting Shapes" on page 41.

You will be cutting these strips and pieces, as needed, for each block. Save the remaining fabrics for additional cutting of sashing and border pieces, as described on page 117.

From the light print, cut:

- 2 strips, 2" [5.5 cm] wide
- 4 strips, 2¾" [7.5 cm] wide
- 1 strip, 3½" [9.5 cm] wide. From this strip, cut a 23" [60 cm]-long piece; trim the remaining shorter length to 3⅛" [8.5 cm] wide.
- 1 strip, 5¾" [15.5 cm] wide. From this strip, cut 1 square, 5¾" x 5 ¾" [15.5 cm x 15.5 cm]; trim the remainder of the strip to 4¼" [11.5 cm] wide.
- Cut an 18" [45 cm] length from the 4¼" [11.5 cm]-wide strip; trim the remainder of the strip to 3⅞" [10.5 cm] wide (It should be at least 16" [40 cm] long.)

From the medium print, cut:

- 1 strip, 2" [5.5 cm] wide
- 2 strips, 2¾" [7.5 cm] wide
- 1 strip, 5⅜" [14.5 cm] wide. From this strip cut 1 square, 5⅜" x 5⅜" [14.5 cm x 14.5 cm], and 1 square, 3½" x 3½" [9.5 cm x 9.5 cm]. Cut the remainder of the strip in half; trim 1 half to 3⅞" [10.5 cm] wide, and the other half to 3⅛" [8.5 cm] wide.

From the dark print, cut:

- 2 strips, 2¾" [7.5 cm] wide
- 1 strip, 3⅞" [10.5 cm] wide. Cut this strip in half; trim 1 half to 3⅛" [8.5 cm] wide.
- 1 strip, 5¾" [15.5 cm] wide. From this strip cut 1 square, 5¾" x 5¾" [15.5 cm x 15.5 cm]; trim the remainder of the strip to 4¼" [11.5 cm] wide.

Making the Blocks

The quilt top is constructed in three stages. First, make the nine blocks. Second, frame the blocks. Third, make the sashing and borders.

 **CHURN DASH
(a Nine-patch block)**

1. Join a 2" [5.5 cm] light strip and a 2" [5.5 cm] medium strip. Press the seam allowance toward the medium fabric. Crosscut the joined strips to make four segments, 3½" x 3½" [9.5 cm x 9.5 cm].

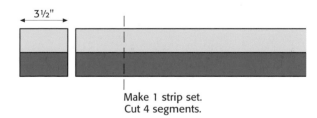

Make 1 strip set.
Cut 4 segments.

2. From the 3½" [9.5 cm] light strip, crosscut one square, 3½" x 3½" [9.5 cm x 9.5 cm], for the center of the block.

3. From the 3⅞" [10.5 cm] dark strip and the 3⅞" [10.5 cm] light strip, crosscut two squares, 3⅞" x 3⅞" [10.5 cm x 10.5 cm], from each strip. Cut the squares across the diagonal to make four half-square triangles of each value.

4. Join the light and dark triangles to make four half-square-triangle units for the block corners.

Make 4.

5. Lay out the block as shown. Join the pieces to make three rows. Press the seam allowances toward the strip-pieced units. Join the three rows and press the completed block.

Churn Dash

 **MILKY WAY
(a Nine-patch block)**

1. From the remainder of the light and medium strip set (see "Churn Dash," step 1), crosscut eight 2" [5.5 cm]-wide segments.

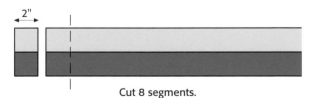

2"

Cut 8 segments.

2. Join the segments to make four-patch units for the block corners. Make four.

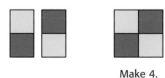

Make 4.

3. From the 3½" [9.5 cm]-wide light strip, cross-cut one square, 3½" x 3½" [9.5 cm x 9.5 cm], for the block center.

4. From the 3⅞" [10.5 cm]-wide dark strip and the 3⅞" [10.5 cm]-wide light strip, crosscut two squares, 3⅞" x 3⅞" [10.5 cm x 10.5], from each strip. Cut squares in half across the diagonal to make four half-square triangles of each value.

5. Join the light and dark triangles to make four half-square-triangle units.

Make 4.

6. Lay out the block as shown. Join the pieces to make three rows. Press seam allowances away from the half-square-triangle units. Join the three rows and press the completed block.

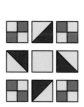 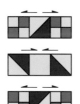

Milky Way

 **OLD MAID'S PUZZLE
(a Four-patch block)**

1. From a 2¾" [7.5 cm]-wide light strip, crosscut four squares, 2¾" x 2¾" [7.5 cm x 7.5 cm].

2. From the 3⅛" [8.5 cm]-wide light strip, crosscut five squares, 3⅛" x 3⅛" [8.5 cm x 8.5 cm]. From the 3⅛" [8.5 cm]-wide dark strip, crosscut three squares, 3⅛" x 3⅛" [8.5 cm x 8.5 cm]. Cut all the squares in half across the diagonal to make 10 light and 6 dark half-square triangles.

3. Join six light triangles to six dark triangles to make six half-square-triangle units.

Make 6.

4. Join the four remaining light triangles to either side of two of the half-square triangle units, as shown, to make two pieced triangles.

Make 2.

5. Cut the 5⅜" [14.5 cm] medium square across the diagonal to make two half-square triangles. Join these triangles to the pieced triangles from step 4.

Make 2.

6. Join the four light squares from step 1 to the remaining four half-square-triangle units. Sew these units together to make two four-patch units.

Make 2.

7. Lay out the block as shown. Join the pieces to make two rows. Press seam allowances toward the medium triangles. Sew the two rows together and press the completed block.

Old Maid's Puzzle

INDIAN STAR
(a Four-patch block)

1. From a 2¾" [7.5 cm]-wide light strip, crosscut six squares, 2¾" x 2¾" [7.5 cm x 7.5 cm].

2. From a 2¾" [7.5 cm]-wide medium strip, crosscut two squares, 2¾" x 2¾" [7.5 cm x 7.5 cm].

3. Join two light squares and two medium squares to make a four-patch unit.

Make 1.

4. From the 2¾" [7.5 cm]-wide light strip, crosscut four rectangles, 2¾" x 5" [7.5 cm x 13.5 cm].

5. From the 2¾" [7.5 cm]-wide dark strip, crosscut eight squares, 2¾" x 2¾" [7.5 cm x 7.5 cm].

6. Using the four light rectangles and the eight dark squares, make four flying-geese units (refer to "Flying Geese" on page 53).

 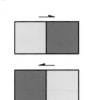

Stitch and trim.   Press.   Make 4.

7. Lay out the block as shown. Join the pieces to make three rows. Press seam allowances away from the flying-geese units. Sew the three rows together and press the completed block.

 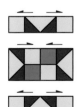

Indian Star

 DUTCHMAN'S PUZZLE
(a Four-patch block)

1. From the 2¾" [7.5 cm]-wide light strips, crosscut 16 squares, 2¾" x 2¾" [7.5 cm x 7.5 cm].

2. From a 2¾" [7.5 cm]-wide dark strip, crosscut four rectangles, 2¾" x 5" [7.5 cm x 13.5 cm].

3. From a 2¾" [7.5 cm]-wide medium strip, crosscut four rectangles, 2¾" x 5" [7.5 cm x 13.5 cm].

4. Using eight of the light squares and four dark rectangles, make four flying-geese units. (Refer to "Flying Geese".) Use the remaining eight light squares and the four medium rectangles to make four flying-geese units.

Make 4.

Make 4.

5. Join the dark and medium flying-geese units in pairs to make four square units. Press the seam allowances toward the medium triangles.

Make 4.

6. Lay out the units as shown. Join the units to make two rows, pressing the seams toward the dark triangles. Join the rows and press the completed block.

Dutchman's Puzzle

SARAH'S CHOICE
(a Four-patch block)

1. From a 2¾" [7.5 cm]-wide light strip, cut four squares, 2¾" x 2¾" [7.5 cm x 7.5 cm].

2. From a 3⅛" [8.5 cm]-wide medium strip, cut two squares, 3⅛" x 3⅛" [8.5 cm x 8.5 cm]. Cut the squares in half across the diagonal to make four half-square triangles.

3. From a 3⅛" [8.5 cm]-wide dark strip, cut two squares, 3⅛" x 3⅛" [8.5 cm x 8.5 cm]. Cut the squares in half across the diagonal to make four half-square triangles.

4. Join the dark and medium half-square triangles to make four half-square-triangle units. Press the seam allowances toward the dark triangles.

5. Lay out the half-square-triangle units as shown. Sew them together in pairs, and then join the two rows to make a pinwheel unit. Note that you will have some bulk at the center of the pinwheel. It's important to pin match the joining seams here to get a nice pointy match. (See "Using Pins" on page 48.)

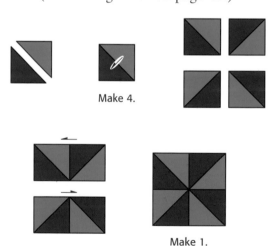

Make 4.

Make 1.

6. From a 2¾" [7.5 cm]-wide light strip, cut four rectangles, 2¾" x 5" [7.5 cm x 13.5 cm].

7. From a 2¾" [7.5 cm]-wide dark strip, cut four squares, 2¾" x 2¾" [7.5 cm x 7.5 cm]. From a

2¾" [7.5 cm]-wide medium strip, cut four squares, 2¾" x 2¾" [7.5 cm x 7.5 cm].

8. Using the light rectangles, dark squares, and medium squares, make four flying-geese units. Each unit should have a dark triangle on the left side and a medium triangle on the right side. (Refer to "Flying Geese" on page 53.)

Make 4.

9. Lay out the block as shown. Join the pieces to make three rows. Press the seam allowance away from the flying-geese units. Join the rows and press the completed block.

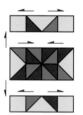 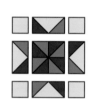

Sarah's Choice

SHOOTING STAR
(a Four-patch block)

1. From a 2¾" [7.5 cm]-wide light strip, cut 12 squares, 2¾" x 2¾" [7.5 cm x 7.5 cm].

2. From a 2¾" [7.5 cm]-wide medium strip, cut four squares, 2¾s x 2¾" [7.5 cm x 7.5 cm].

3. Join four of the light squares to the four medium squares in pairs.

Make 4.

4. From a 2¾" [7.5 cm]-wide dark strip, cut four rectangles, 2¾" x 5" [7.5 cm x 13.5 cm].

5. Using the eight remaining light squares and the four dark rectangles, make four parallelograms (refer to "Parallelograms" on page 54).

Note that the seams for the parallelograms must all be stitched in the same direction as shown.

Make 4.

6. Lay out the block as shown. Join the paired squares to the parallelograms to make four larger pieced squares. Press the seam allowances toward the squares.

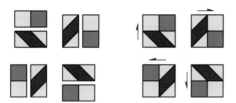

7. Join the square units to make two rows, pressing the seam allowances away from the dark parallelograms. Join the rows and press the completed block.

Shooting Star

OHIO STAR
(a Nine-patch block)

1. From a 3½" [9.5 cm]-wide light strip, cut four squares, 3½" x 3½" [9.5 cm x 9.5 cm].

2. From the light and dark 4¼" [11.5 cm]-wide strips, crosscut four squares, 4¼" x 4¼" [11.5 cm x 11.5 cm], from each strip. Cut the squares in half across both diagonals (being careful not to move the pieces between the first and second cut) to make eight quarter-square triangles of each value.

3. Join the dark and light quarter-square triangles to make four quarter-square-triangle units. Press the seam allowances toward the dark triangles.

Make 8.   Make 4.

4. Using the quarter-square-triangle units, the 3½" [9.5 cm] light squares, and the previously cut 3½" [9.5 cm] medium square, lay out the block as shown. Join the pieces to make three rows, and press the seam allowances toward the squares. Join the rows and press the completed block.

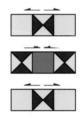 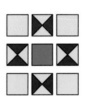

Ohio Star

PINWHEEL II
(a Four-patch block)

1. From a 2" [5.5 cm]-wide light strip, cut four rectangles, 2" x 5" [5.5 cm x 13.5].

2. From a 3⅞" [10.5 cm]-wide medium strip, cut two squares, 3⅞" x 3⅞" [10.5 cm x 10.5 cm]. Cut the squares in half across the diagonal to make four half-square triangles.

3. Join the four light rectangles to the four medium triangles, as shown. Trim the corners of the rectangles on the diagonal, even with the diagonal edges of the triangles.

Make 4.

4. Cut the light and dark 5¾" [15.5 cm] squares in half across both diagonals to make four quarter-square triangles of each value.

5. Join the light and dark triangles to make four larger pieced triangles, as shown.

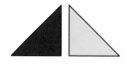

Make 4.

6. Lay out the block pieces as shown. Join the two different triangle units into pairs, making four pieced squares. Press the seam allowances toward the dark triangles.

Make 4.

7. Join the pieced squares to make two rows. Since you've pressed all the seams toward the dark triangles, the allowances on the diagonal seams should butt neatly together when you place the squares on top of each other.

8. Join the rows, using a pin to match the center where eight triangle points all meet. (See "Using Pins" on page 48.) Press the completed block.

Pinwheel II

Framing the Blocks

Each of the nine blocks should measure 9½" [25.5 cm] square. But don't panic if they are not exactly the right size. This quilt has been designed with framing strips around each block that enable you to make all your blocks exactly the right size.

1. From the medium print, cut nine strips, 1¾" [4.5 cm] wide. Working with one block at a time, measure the block through the center to find the exact length and crosscut the framing strip to make two pieces this length. Join these strips to opposite sides of the block, pressing the seam allowances toward the strips. Measure the block through its width, including the newly added strips, and crosscut two strips to this length. Join these strips to the top and bottom of the block and press the seam allowances toward the strips.

2. Matching the center of the block with the 5½" [14.25 cm] line on your large square ruler, trim each block to 11" [28.5 cm] square. (To find the center of a Nine Patch block, fold the block into quarters and finger-press the center fold to mark the center point.)

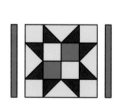 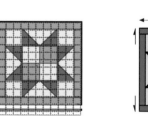

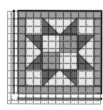

Trim to 11" [28.5 cm] square.

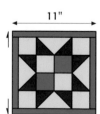

11"

Cutting Sashing, Borders, and Binding

Cut across the width of the fabric unless otherwise specified.

From the dark print, cut on the lengthwise grain, referring to "Cutting Lengthwise Strips" on page 43:

- 4 strips, 5" [13.5 cm] wide x length of fabric

- 4 strips, 1⅝" [4.5 cm] wide x length of fabric; crosscut into 128 squares, 1⅝" x 1⅝" [4.5 cm x 4.5 cm].

- 4 binding strips, 2½" [7 cm] wide x length of fabric

From the light print, cut:

- 8 strips, 2¾" [7.5 cm] wide. From each strip, crosscut three strips, 2¾" x 11" [7.5 cm x 28.5 cm], to make 24 total. From the remainders of the strips, cut 16 squares, 2¾" x 2¾" [7.5 cm x 7.5 cm].

From the medium print, cut:

- 5 strips, 2¾" [7.5 cm] wide. From each of four strips, crosscut three strips, 2¾" x 11" [7.5 cm x 28.5 cm], to make 12 total. From the remainders of the strips, cut 20 squares, 2¾" x 2¾" [7.5 cm x 7.5 cm].

Adding Sashing and Borders

1. Using a pencil and ruler, mark a diagonal line on the wrong side of each dark 1⅝" [4.5 cm] square. If necessary, use a silver pencil or chalk wheel to make the markings visible.

2. To make the pieced sashing strips, join a dark square to each corner of each light 2¾" x 11" [7.5 cm x 28.5 cm] sashing strip, referring to "Snowball Blocks" on page 54. Trim away the excess fabric in the corners and press the dark triangle open. It is easiest to chain-piece the same corner on each of the strips, trim and press them open, and then continue with the next corner in the same manner until all corners are completed.

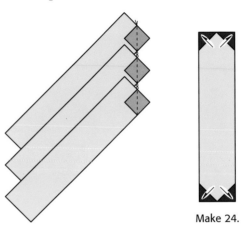

Make 24.

3. To make the pieced squares in the first border, join the remaining small dark squares to two adjacent corners of each of 16 medium squares as you did for the rectangles in step 2 above. Trim each corner and press open.

Make 16.

4. Lay out the quilt blocks, sashing, pieced squares, and cornerstones as shown. Sew the pieces together into rows. Press the seam allowances away from the corner triangles of sashing, which means you'll press the seams

toward the blocks, the medium sashing strips, and the plain cornerstones.

5. Join the block and sashing rows, pressing seam allowances toward the sashing rows.

6. Using two of the dark border strips, square up one end of each strip. Measure the strips to fit the length of the quilt, referring to "Butted Corners" on page 73. Cut strips to this length. Pin and sew the border strips to the quilt sides. Press the seam allowances toward the borders.

7. Square up one end of each of the two remaining dark border strips. Measure the strips to fit the width of the quilt, again referring to "Butted Corners." Cut strips to this length.

Pin and sew them to the top and bottom of the quilt. Press the seam allowances toward the borders.

Quilting

1. Cut the backing fabric in half and join the two pieces side by side. Trim the backing to 58" [150 cm] square.

2. Layer the backing, batting, and quilt top, referring to "Layering" on page 78.

3. Baste the layers together, referring to "Pin Basting" on page 79 if you'll be machine quilting or "Thread Basting" on page 79 if you'll be hand quilting.

4. Quilt as desired. One suggestion is to outline quilt the borders, sashing, and framing strips. Outline quilt around the triangle points in the sashing and the pieces in each block. Add straight lines in borders.

Finishing

Attach the binding to your quilt, referring to "Binding" on page 90.

Piecing Sampler Variation

This pretty quilt has a much softer look than the version shown on page 109

because the contrast between the color values is not as strong.

COSMOS by Margaret Rolfe

Snowball and Nine Patch

BRING ON THE CLOWNS by Jenny Bowker

An easy-to-make quilt for a baby or toddler, this project uses simple, quick-piecing techniques, including strip piecing and stitch-and-fold corners. Choose the fabrics by first selecting a main fabric for the Snowball blocks and outer border. Look for a charming children's print. Then look for the coordinating fabrics— a light and a medium print for the Nine Patch blocks, and a dark print for the corners of the Snowball blocks, inner border, and binding.

Size of quilt top: 44½" x 56½" [111.5 cm x 141.5 cm]
Finished block size: 6" [15 cm]

Nine Patch Block

Snowball Block

Materials

Amounts are based on 42" [106 cm]-wide fabric.

- 1½ yards [1.4 m] of main fabric for Snowball blocks and outer border

- 1 yard [1 m] of dark print for Snowball blocks, inner border, and binding

- ½ yard [50 cm] of light print for Nine Patch blocks

- ½ yard [50 cm] of medium print for Nine Patch blocks

- 3 yards [2.5 m] of backing fabric

- 48" x 60" [120 cm x 150 cm] piece of batting

Cutting

Cut across the width of the fabric unless otherwise specified.

From the medium print, cut:

- 6 strips, 2½" [6.5 cm] wide

From the light print, cut:

- 5 strips, 2½" [6.5 cm] wide

From the dark print, cut:

- 5 strips, 2½" [6.5 cm] wide; crosscut into 68 squares, 2½" x 2½" [6.5 cm x 6.5 cm]. (Cut 16 squares from 4 strips, and 4 squares from the fifth strip.) Trim the remainder of the fifth strip to 1½" [4 cm] wide.

- 4 strips, 1½" [4 cm] wide

- 6 strips, 2½" [7 cm] wide

From the main fabric, cut on the lengthwise grain, referring to "Cutting Lengthwise Strips" on page 43:

- 6 strips, 6½" [16.5 cm] wide x length of fabric. Crosscut 2 of the strips into 14 squares, 6½" x 6½" [16.5 cm x 16.5 cm]. From 3 of the remaining strips, cut 1 square, 6½" x 6½" [16.5 cm x 16.5 cm], from each strip. (You now have 17 squares and 4 long strips.)

Making the Nine Patch Blocks

1. Using four medium print strips and two light print strips, join the strips to make two strip sets as shown, with the light print in the center and the medium print on either side. Press the seam allowances toward the medium print strips.

Make 2 strip sets.

2. Using one medium print strip and two light print strips, join the strips to make one strip set with the medium print in the center and the light print on either side. Press the seam allowances toward the medium print strips.

Make 1 strip set.

3. Cut the remaining medium print strip into two 12" [31 cm] lengths and one 7" [18 cm] length.

4. Cut the remaining light print strip into one 12" [31 cm] length and two 7" [18 cm] lengths.

5. Join these lengths to make two strip sets, a shorter one with the light print on the outside and a longer one with the medium print on the outside. Press the seam allowances toward the medium print strips.

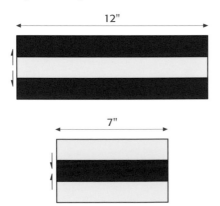

6. Crosscut all strip sets into 2½" [6.5 cm] segments, cutting a total of 36 segments with the light print in the center and 18 segments with the medium print in the center.

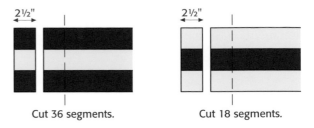

Cut 36 segments.   Cut 18 segments.

7. Sew the units together to make 18 Nine Patch blocks.

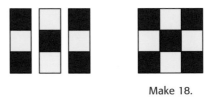

Make 18.

Making the Snowball Blocks

Using the 68 small dark squares and the 17 large squares of main fabric, make 17 Snowball blocks. (See "Snowball Blocks" on page 54.)

Make 17.

Assembling the Quilt

1. Lay out the Nine Patch and Snowball blocks as shown, making sure all blocks are oriented correctly. This is especially important if your main fabric is a directional print and you want all the blocks to be facing in the same direction. Join the blocks into seven rows. Press the

seam allowances toward the Nine Patch blocks.

2. Sew the rows together to make the quilt center.

Adding the Borders

1. Cut the short 1½" [4 cm]-wide dark print strip for the inner border in half. Join each half to a full-length strip to make two long border strips. Square up one end of each strip. Measure the strips to fit the length of the quilt, referring to "Butted Corners" on page 73. Cut the strips to this length. Pin and sew the border strips to the quilt sides. Press the seam allowances toward the borders.

2. Square up one end of each of the two remaining 1½" [4 cm] inner-border strips. Measure the strips to fit the width of the quilt, again referring to "Butted Corners." Cut strips to this length. Pin and sew them to the top and bottom of the quilt. Press the seam allowances toward the borders.

3. Using the four 6½" [16.5 cm]-wide main fabric strips, add the outer border, measuring the strips to the correct lengths as described in steps 1 and 2 above.

Quilting

1. Cut the backing fabric in half and join the two pieces side by side. The backing will have a horizontal seam. Trim the backing to 61" [150 cm] long.

2. Layer the backing, batting, and quilt top, referring to "Layering" on page 78.

3. Baste the layers together, referring to "Pin Basting" on page 79 if you'll be machine quilting or "Thread Basting" on page 79 if you'll be hand quilting.

4. Quilt as desired. We suggest outline quilting the blocks, borders, and shapes within the blocks. For the Snowball blocks and border, quilt straight lines following the lines of the Nine Patch blocks or free-motion machine quilt a meandering pattern.

Finishing

Review "Binding" on page 90.

1. Cut two of the binding strips in half. Join each half to a full strip to make two longer strips for the sides.

2. Attach the binding to your quilt.

Snowball and Nine Patch Variation

You can vary this design just by changing the placement of the light and medium fabrics in the Nine Patch blocks. In the quilt shown here, the light fabric is in the corners of the blocks, while in the project quilt shown on page 120, the medium fabric is in the corners.

TUMBLING TEDDIES by Jenny Bowker

Friendship Star

HARRY'S QUILT by Jenny Bowker

Simple squares, rectangles, and half-square triangles combine for a complex-looking quilt that's actually easy to make. In addition to the Friendship Star blocks, more stars are cleverly formed through the use of pieced sashing and cornerstones. The background for this quilt can be either light or dark. For the star points in the blocks and sashing, choose fabrics that will contrast with the background, though you may wish to have a little less contrast in the sashing star points to add subtlety to the design.

Size of quilt top: 53½" x 63½" [129.5 cm x 153.5 cm]
Finished block size: 7½" [18 cm]

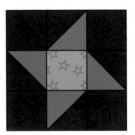

Friendship Star Block

Materials

Amounts are based on 42" [106 cm]-wide fabric.

- 1⅝ yards [1.4 m] of bold print for outer border and binding (You may want to choose this fabric after you have completed the center of the quilt.)
- 1¾ yards [1.6 m] of print for background (light or dark)
- ½ yard [40 cm] of contrast print for block star points
- ½ yard [40 cm] of second contrast print for sashing star points

- ⅓ yard [30 cm] of print for inner border
- ¼ yard [20 cm] or fat quarter of print for block centers
- 4½" [10 cm]-wide strip or fat eighth of print for sashing cornerstones
- 3¼ yards [2.9 m] of backing fabric
- 57" x 67" [138 cm x 162 cm] piece of batting

Cutting

Cut across the width of the fabric unless otherwise specified.

From the background fabric, cut:
- 4 strips, 7½" [19 cm] wide; crosscut into 16 squares, 7 ½" x 7 ½" [19 cm x 19 cm]
- 10 strips, 3" [7.5 cm] wide; crosscut 2 strips into 14 rectangles, 3" x 5½" [7.5 cm x 13.5 cm], and crosscut the remaining strips to make 97 squares, 3" x 3" [7.5 cm x 7.5 cm]

From the contrast print, cut:
- 2 strips, 7½" [19 cm] wide; crosscut into 10 squares, 7½" x 7½" [19 cm x 19 cm]

From the second contrast print, cut:
- 2 strips, 7½" [19 cm] wide; crosscut into 6 squares, 7½" x 7½" [19 cm x 19 cm]

From the print for block centers, cut:
- 2 strips, 3" [7.5 cm] wide; crosscut into 20 squares, 3" x 3" [7.5 cm x 7.5 cm]

From the print for sashing cornerstones, cut:
- 1 strip, 3" [7.5 cm] wide; crosscut into 12 squares, 3" x 3" [7.5 cm x 7.5 cm]

From the print for inner border, cut:
- 5 strips, 1¾" [4.5 cm] wide

From the bold print, cut on the lengthwise grain, referring to "Cutting Lengthwise Strips" on page 43:
- 4 strips, 7" [17.5 cm] wide x length of fabric
- 5 strips, 2½" [7 cm] wide x length of fabric

Making the Half-Square Triangle Units

Because this quilt uses so many identical half-square-triangle units, we find it easiest to make them in batches using the method shown on page 50.

1. Using 10 each of the 7½" [19 cm] background fabric squares and contrast print squares, make 80 half-square-triangle units. Each pair of contrast print and background fabric squares will yield eight finished half-square-triangle units. Trim the units to 3" [7.5 cm] square.

 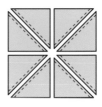

Make 80.

2. Using six each of the 7½" [19 cm] background fabric squares and second contrast print squares, make 48 half-square-triangle units. Trim the units to 3" [7.5 cm] square.

 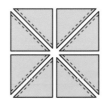

Make 48.

Making the Friendship Star Blocks

1. Lay out four half-square-triangle units for block star points, four 3" [7.5 cm] background squares, and one 3" [7.5 cm] block center square to make a Friendship Star block.

2. Join the units into rows and press the seams toward the plain squares.

3. Join the rows and press the completed block. Repeat these steps to make 20 Friendship Star blocks.

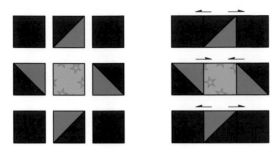

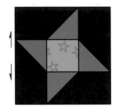

Friendship Star
Make 20.

Piecing the Sashing

1. Using the half-square-triangle units for sashing star points and 3" [7.5 cm] background squares, make 17 pieced sashing strips for the quilt center, as shown. Press the seam allowances toward the plain squares.

Make 17.

2. Using the remaining half-square-triangle units and 3" x 5½" [7.5 cm x 13.5 cm] background fabric rectangles, make 14 pieced sashing strips for the outer edge of the quilt center, as shown. Press the seam allowances toward the rectangles.

Make 14.

Assembling the Quilt

1. Lay out the Friendship Star blocks, pieced sashing strips, and corner squares, as shown. Be careful to place the pieced sashing strips so that stars will form in the interior of the quilt and you won't have stray triangles at the edges of the quilt.

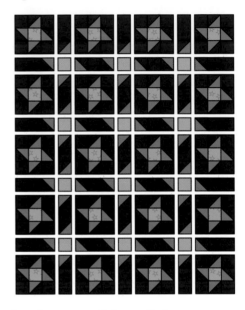

2. Join the elements of the quilt into rows, pressing the seam allowances in alternate directions, as shown.

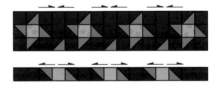

3. Join the rows to make the quilt center.

Adding the Borders

1. Cut one of the inner-border strips in half and join each half-strip to another full-length strip to make two long inner-border strips. Square up one end of each strip. Measure the strips to fit the length of the quilt, referring to "Butted Corners" on page 73. Cut strips to this length. Pin and sew the border strips to opposite sides of the quilt. Press the seam allowances toward the borders.

2. Square up one end of each of the two remaining inner-border strips. Measure the strips to fit the width of the quilt, again referring to "Butted Corners." Cut the strips to this length. Pin and sew them to the top and bottom of the quilt. Press the seam allowances toward the borders.

3. Using the four 7" [17.5 cm]-wide bold print strips, add the outer border, measuring the strips to the correct lengths as described in steps 1 and 2 above.

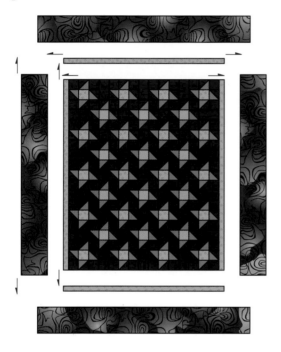

Quilting

1. Cut the fabric for the backing in half and join the two pieces side by side. Trim the backing to 67" [162 cm] long; your backing will have a horizontal seam.

2. Layer the backing, batting, and quilt top, referring to "Layering" on page 78.

3. Baste the layers together, referring to "Pin Basting" on page 79 if you'll be machine quilting or "Thread Basting" on page 79 if you'll be hand quilting.

4. Quilt as desired. We suggest outline quilting the borders and free-motion quilting spirals in the quilt center and outer border.

Finishing

Review "Binding" on page 90.

1. Cut one of the binding strips in half. Join these half strips to two of the remaining full-length strips to make longer strips for the sides.

2. Attach the binding to your quilt.

Friendship Star Variation

The beautiful autumn colors of the stars in this quilt are taken from the wonderful large-scale border print. Notice how different this quilt looks from the one shown on page 125, largely due to the use of a light background fabric instead of a dark one.

SEASON OF MISTS by Jenny Bowker

LION AROUND by Jenny Bowker

This quilt stars a feature theme-print fabric and a stripe; it will give you experience in using directional fabrics. While there is a lot of movement in the design, the quilt is made of simple components: Puss in the Corner blocks, alternate blocks of feature fabric, and sashing made of four-patch and flying-geese units.

The design on your feature fabric will determine how you want to use it; we wanted to keep the faces of the animals all going in the same direction. Choose the feature fabric and then select coordinating fabrics—a bright accent fabric, a stripe for the blocks and inner border, a light and a dark for the sashing, and a medium to go with the bright accent in the four-patch corners. We finished off our quilt with more of the stripe used for binding, but you may want to make that decision after the borders have been added.

Size of quilt top: 56½" x 56½" [141.5 cm x 141.5 cm]
Finished block size: 8" [20 cm]

Puss in the Corner Block

Materials

Amounts are based on 42" [106 cm]-wide fabric.

- 2 yards [1.7 m] of feature fabric
- ¾ yard [70 cm] of dark print for flying-geese units in sashing
- ¾ yard [70 cm] of light print for flying-geese units in sashing
- ⅝ yard [60 cm] of striped print for blocks and inner border

- ⅓ yard [30 cm] of bright accent print for blocks and sashing
- ¼ yard [20 cm] of medium print for sashing
- ½ yard [50 cm] of print for binding
- 3½ yards [3.1 m] of backing fabric
- 60" x 60" [150 cm x 150 cm] piece of batting

Cutting

Cut across the width of the fabric unless otherwise specified.

From the feature fabric, cut:
- 3 border strips, 6½" [16.5 cm] wide

From the remaining feature fabric, cut on the lengthwise grain:
- 2 border strips, 6½" [16.5 cm] wide
- 1 strip, 8½" [21.5 cm] wide; crosscut into 4 squares, 8½" x 8½" [21.5 cm x 21.5 cm]
- 1 strip, 4½" [11.5 cm] wide; crosscut into 5 squares, 4½" x 4½" [11.5 cm x 11.5 cm]

From the dark print, cut:
- 5 strips, 4½" [11.5 cm] wide; crosscut into 40 squares, 4½" x 4½" [11.5 cm x 11.5 cm]

From the light print, cut:
- 5 strips, 4½" [11.5 cm] wide; crosscut into 20 rectangles, 4½" x 8½" [11.5 cm x 21.5 cm]

From the striped print, cut:
- 4 strips, 2½" [6.5 cm] wide
- 3 strips, 2½" [6.5 cm] wide; crosscut into 20 rectangles, 2½" x 4½" [6.5 cm x 11.5 cm]

From the bright print, cut:
- 4 strips, 2½" [6.5 cm] wide; crosscut 2 of the strips into 24 squares, 2½" x 2½" [6.5 cm x 6.5 cm]

From the medium print, cut:
- 2 strips, 2½" [6.5 cm] wide

From the binding print, cut:
- 6 strips, 2½" [7 cm] wide

Making the Puss in the Corner Blocks

1. Sew a bright print square to each end of 10 of the striped rectangles. Press seams toward the bright print.

Make 10.

2. Sew the remaining 10 striped rectangles to the sides of the 4½" [11.5 cm] feature fabric squares. Press the seam allowances toward the feature fabric.

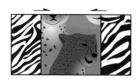

Make 5.

3. Join the units from steps 1 and 2 to make five Puss in the Corner blocks.

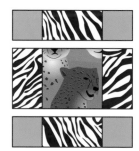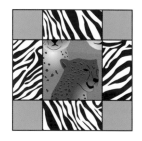

Puss in the Corner
Make 5.

Making the Sashing

1. For the flying-geese units, sew the dark print squares to the light print rectangles, referring to "Flying Geese" on page 53. Make 20 units.

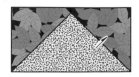

Make 20.

2. For the four-patch units, sew together the bright print and medium print strips lengthwise in pairs to make two strip sets. Press the seam allowances toward the medium print.

Make 2 strip sets.

3. Square up the end of each strip set, and crosscut each into 16 segments, 2½" [6.5 cm] wide.

2½"

Cut 32 segments.

4. Sew the segments together in pairs to make 16 Four Patch blocks.

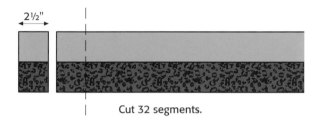

Make 16.

Assembling the Quilt

1. Lay out the Puss in the Corner blocks, the 8½" [21.5 cm] feature fabric squares, the flying-geese sashing, and the four-patch cornerstones, as shown. Place the four-patch cornerstones carefully, so that the bright squares radiate out from the pieced blocks. Make sure the feature fabric blocks are all oriented cor-

rectly. Note how the flying geese create a diamond around the Puss in the Corner blocks.

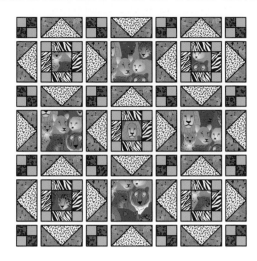

2. Join the elements of the quilt into rows. In the rows of four-patch cornerstones and flying-geese sashing, press the seams toward the four-patch cornerstones. In the blocks and sashing rows, press the seams toward the blocks.

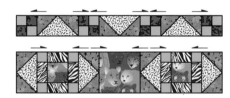

3. Join the rows to make the quilt center. Press.

Adding the Borders

1. Square up one end of each striped print inner-border strip. Measure and cut two strips to the width of the quilt and two strips to the length of the quilt, referring to "Corner Squares" on page 74. Join the two strips measured for the length to the sides of the quilt. Press the seam allowances toward the borders.

2. Join the remaining bright print squares to the ends of the remaining two border strips.

Attach the strips to the top and bottom of the quilt. Press the seam allowances toward the borders.

3. Square up one end on each of two feature fabric outer-border strips that were cut on the lengthwise grain. Measure the strips to fit the length of the quilt, again referring to "Butted Corners" on page 73. Cut the strips to this length. Pin and sew to the quilt sides. Press the seam allowances toward the borders.

4. Cut one of the remaining feature fabric border strips in half. Join each half to one of the remaining full-length strips to make two long borders. (Some extra fabric has been allowed for matching the design on the fabric, but it does not have to match exactly. See "Crosswise vs. Lengthwise Borders," page 71.)

5. Square up one end of each border strip. Measure the strips to fit the width of your quilt. Cut strips to this length. Pin and sew them to the top and bottom of the quilt. Press the seam allowances toward the borders.

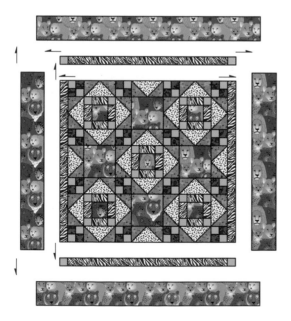

Quilting

1. Cut the backing fabric in half and join the two pieces side by side. Trim the backing to 60" [150 cm] square.

2. Layer the backing, batting, and quilt top, referring to "Layering" on page 78.

3. Baste the layers together, referring to "Pin Basting" on page 79 if you'll be machine quilting or "Thread Basting" on page 79 if you'll be hand quilting.

4. Quilt as desired. We suggest outline quilting the inner border and corner squares, and then quilting the quilt center and borders with free-motion loops.

Finishing

Review "Binding" on page 90.

1. Cut two of the binding strips in half to make four half strips. Join these half strips to the four remaining strips to make four long strips.

2. Attach the binding to your quilt.

Feature Fabric Variation

Notice how in this variation of the same quilt pattern, a directional fabric for the border is cut so that the print circles around the quilt, with each piece facing toward the center rather than all facing vertically. The look of the finished project is quite different from the original one shown on page 130.

CRANES OVER THE MOUNTAINS by Jenny Bowker

Log Cabin

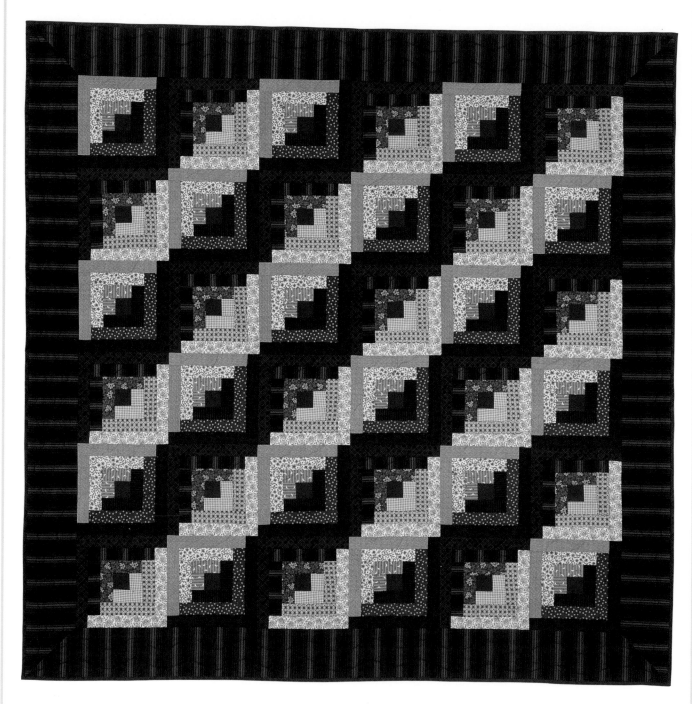

STARS, STRIPES, AND FURROWS by Jenny Bowker

In this Log Cabin design, we used a traditional Straight Furrows setting that showcases the light and dark fabrics in diagonal bands, even though the blocks are set side by side, not on point. We chose a striped border and mitered the corners, but squared corners could be used if a different print were chosen.

Size of quilt top: 78½" x 78½" [199.5 cm x 199.5 cm]
Finished block size: 11" [29 cm]

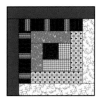

Log Cabin Block

Materials

Amounts are based on 42" [106 cm]-wide fabric.

This quilt is constructed from two repeating blocks, so you will need two sets of fabric, each consisting of three different lights and three different darks. The center squares are the same in all blocks. Choose six light and six dark prints, and a red print or solid for the center squares. When selecting fabrics for the logs, make groups of the light fabrics and dark fabrics to see how they work together. While maintaining the contrast between the light and dark, remember to have each print differ a little from its neighbor to add interest. Don't over-match.

- 1⅝ yards [1.3 m] of print for the border
- ¾ yard [70 cm] each of 2 different dark prints for third round of dark logs
- ½ yard [50 cm] each of 2 different dark prints for second round of dark logs
- ⅓ yard [40 cm] each of 2 different dark prints for first round of dark logs
- ⅝ yard [60 cm] each of 2 different light prints for third round of light logs
- ½ yard [50 cm] each of 2 different light prints for second round of light logs
- ¼ yard [30 cm] each of 2 different light prints for first round of light logs
- ¼ yard [30 cm] of red print for center squares
- ⅝ yard [60 cm] of print for binding
- 4¾ yards [4.4 m] of backing fabric
- 82" x 82" [214 cm x 214 cm] piece of batting

Cutting

Cut across the width of the fabric. Once it is cut, you may want to put each size log into a zipper-top plastic bag and label it (Round 1, log 1; Round 1, log 2, etc.) to prevent confusion later.

From the red print for center squares, cut:
*   3 strips, 2½" [6.5 cm] wide; crosscut into 36 squares, 2½" x 2½" [6.5 cm x 6.5 cm]

From *both* prints for first-round light logs, cut:
*   3 strips, 2" [5.5 cm] wide; crosscut each set of strips into 18 rectangles, 2½" [6.5 cm] long, and 18 rectangles, 4" [10.5 cm] long

From *both* prints for first-round dark logs, cut:
*   5 strips, 2" [5.5 cm] wide; crosscut each set of strips into 18 rectangles, 4" [10.5 cm] long, and 18 rectangles, 5½" [14.5 cm] long

From *both* prints for second-round light logs, cut:
*   7 strips, 2" [5.5 cm] wide; crosscut each set of strips into 18 rectangles, 5½" [14.5 cm] long, and 18 rectangles, 7" [18.5 cm] long

From *both* prints for second-round dark logs, cut:
*   8 strips, 2" [5.5 cm] wide; crosscut each set of strips into 18 rectangles, 7" [18.5 cm] long, and 18 rectangles, 8½" [22.5 cm] long

From *both* prints for third-round light logs, cut:
*   9 strips, 2" [5.5 cm] wide; crosscut each set of strips into 18 rectangles, 8½" [22.5 cm] long, and 18 rectangles, 10" [26.5 cm] long

From *both* prints for third-round dark logs, cut:
*   11 strips, 2" [5.5 cm] wide; crosscut each set of strips into 18 rectangles, 10" [26.5 cm] long, and 18 rectangles, 11½" [30.5 cm] long

From the print for border, cut:
*   8 strips, 6½" [13.5 cm] wide

From the print for binding, cut:
*   8 strips, 2½" [7 cm] wide

Making the Log Cabin Blocks

Using the cut squares and rectangles, make 18 blocks from one set of light and dark prints and 18 blocks from the other set, referring to "Piecing Log Cabin Blocks" on page 55.

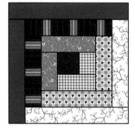 

Make 18.   Make 18.

Assembling the Quilt

1. Lay out the Log Cabin blocks in six rows of six blocks each, alternating the two different blocks throughout the quilt, as shown. Make sure you orient the blocks to make diagonal bands of light and dark.

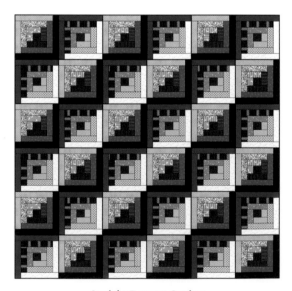

Straight Furrows Setting

2. Join the blocks into rows, pressing the seams in alternate directions from row to row.

3. Join the rows to make the quilt center.

Adding the Borders

1. Join the border strips in pairs to make four long strips, matching the print or stripe as required

2. Add the border to the quilt, referring to "Mitered Corners" on page 75.

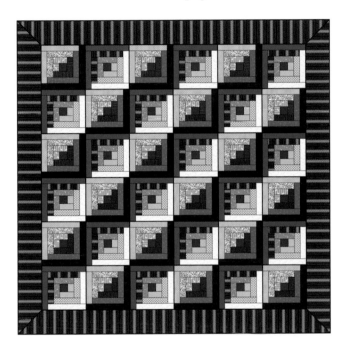

Quilting

1. Cut the backing fabric in half and join the two pieces side by side.

2. Layer the backing, batting, and quilt top, referring to "Layering" on page 78.

3. Baste the layers together, referring to "Pin Basting" on page 79 if you'll be machine quilting or "Thread Basting" on page 79 if you'll be hand quilting.

4. Quilt as desired. We suggest quilting in the ditch around the inner edge of the border and then quilting wavy lines diagonally across the quilt center and around the border.

Finishing

Review "Binding" on page 90.

1. Join the binding strips in pairs to make four long strips.

2. Attach the binding to your quilt.

Log Cabin Variation

This pretty Log Cabin quilt is set in the Barn Raising design. Three kinds of prints were used: a red floral for the block centers, assorted florals for the light logs, and assorted foliage designs for the dark logs and border. The border corners are butted.

CABIN IN THE GARDEN by Jenny Bowker

SUMMER GARDEN by Jenny Bowker

Four lovely flower designs are perfect for practicing your appliqué skills. This quilt also teaches you how to make a quilt with blocks set on point. The setting triangles and the half Nine Patch blocks combine to mimic the look of a white picket fence surrounding a cottage garden.

Size of quilt top: 43" x 43" [109 cm x 109 cm]
Finished block size: 6" [15 cm]

Nine Patch Block

Materials

Amounts are based on 42"[106 cm]-wide fabric.

- 1¼ yards [1.1 m] of cream solid for background

- 1 yard [1 m] of dark green print for Nine Patch blocks and binding

- ⅝ yard [50 cm] of light green print for Nine Patch blocks

- 1 fat quarter or 6" [15 cm] strip each of 12 tone-on-tone prints for flowers, including yellow; gold; orange; light and dark blue; light, medium, and dark purple; pink; rose; dark red; and green

- 2 yards [1.7 m] of backing fabric

- 47" x 47" [118 cm x 118 cm] piece of batting

Cutting

From the background fabric, cut:

- 2 strips, 7" [18 cm] wide; crosscut into 9 squares, 7" x 7" [18 cm x 18 cm]

- 2 strips, 9¾" [25 cm] wide; crosscut into 7 squares, 9¾" x 9¾" [25 cm x 25 cm]. Cut squares in half across both diagonals to make 28 quarter-square triangles.

- 1 strip, 5⅛" [13.5 cm] wide; crosscut into 2 squares, 5⅛" x 5⅛" [13.5 cm x 13.5 cm]. Cut squares in half diagonally to make 4 half-square triangles.

From the dark green print, cut:

- 8 strips, 2½" [6.5 cm] wide; crosscut 1 strip to make 2 pieces, 2½" x 12" [6.5 cm x 30 cm]. Crosscut the remainder of this strip and 1 other strip to make 20 squares, 2½" x 2½" [6.5 cm x 6.5 cm].

- 5 strips, 2½" [7 cm] wide

From the light green print, cut:

- 7 strips, 2½" [6.5 cm] wide; crosscut 1 strip to make 1 piece, 2½" x 12" [6.5 cm x 30 cm]. Crosscut the remainder of this strip and 3 more strips to make 52 squares, 2½" x 2½" [6.5 cm x 6.5 cm].

From *each* of the 12 colored prints for appliqué, cut:

- 3 squares, 2½" x 2½" [6.5 cm x 6.5 cm], to make 36 total

Appliquéing the Flower Blocks

Review "Hand Appliqué" on page 60.

1. Fold the background squares in half on the diagonal in each direction and crease the folds to mark the center of the block. Note that the background squares are cut oversized, so it's important that you center your appliqué motifs as we will be trimming the blocks smaller when they're complete.

2. Trace the rose, daisy, pansy, and iris appliqué patterns (pages 145–146) onto template plastic using black fine-point permanent marker. Trace the patterns lightly onto background squares using pencil, matching the center points.

3. Prepare the appliqué shapes as described on page 61, using the following color guide or making your own color combinations.

   Rose 1: Pink, rose, dark purple, and green

   Rose 2: Yellow, golden yellow, orange, and green

   Rose 3: Rose, orange, yellow, and green

   Daisy 1: Yellow and green

   Daisy 2: Pink and green

   Pansy 1: Dark blue, light blue, yellow, gold, and green

   Pansy 2: Dark blue, light blue, yellow, gold, and green

   Iris 1: Light blue, dark purple, medium purple, and green

   Iris 2: Medium purple, rose, dark purple, and green

   For flower stems, cut bias strips (see page 43) from the green print. For daisies, cut 2 strips, each ¾" [2 cm] wide and 3" [7.5 cm] long. For Irises, cut 2 strips, each ¾" [2 cm] wide and 3¼" [8 cm] long.

4. Appliqué the flowers onto the background blocks in numerical order.

5. Press the completed blocks and trim them to 6½" [16.5 cm] square by matching the center of the block with the 3¼" [8.25 cm] marking on a square ruler.

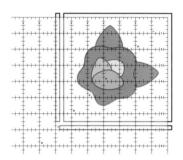

Making the Nine Patch Blocks

1. Using six strips of the dark green print and three strips of the light green print, join the dark green strips to either side of the light green strips to make three strip sets, as shown. Join two dark green 2½" x 12" [30 cm] strips and one light green 2½" x 12" [30 cm] strip to make a short pieced length.

Make 3 strip sets.

Make 1 strip set.

2. Square up the end of each strip set, and cross-cut the strips into 52 segments, 2½" [6.5 cm] wide.

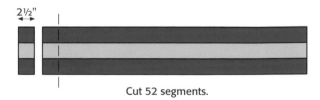

2½"

Cut 52 segments.

3. Sew a 2½" [6.5 cm] light green square to opposite sides of 16 assorted-color 2½" [6.5 cm] squares.

Make 16.

4. Join the light-and-dark-green segments from step 2 to either side of the segments from step 3 to make 16 Nine Patch blocks.

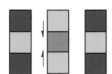

Make 16.

5. Using the remaining light-and-dark-green segments, and the leftover green and assorted-color squares, assemble 20 half Nine Patch blocks, as shown.

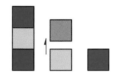

Make 20.

Assembling the Quilt

1. Lay out the Nine Patch blocks, the appliqué flower blocks, 12 of the quarter-square triangles, and the four half-square triangles, as shown. Distribute the colors around the quilt and rearrange until you are satisfied with the layout.

2. Join the blocks and triangles into diagonal rows. Press the seam allowances toward the background fabric.

3. Join the rows to make the quilt center. Press.

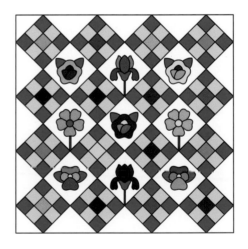

Adding the Border

1. Join the half blocks and side triangles as shown to make four border strips. Note that the borders will have jagged edges.

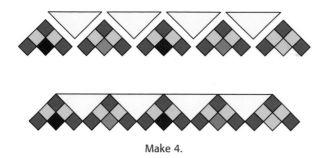

Make 4.

2. Carefully sew a line of stay stitching (machine stitching at normal stitch length) along the outer edge of each border, ⅛" [3 mm] from the inside corners of the squares, as shown. Take care not to stretch the borders as you sew. The point of stay stitching is to prevent the fabrics from stretching as you handle them. This is important because the jagged edges of the borders will be trimmed, leaving bias-cut edges along the outside perimeter of the quilt top.

Stay stitch border edges.

3. Trim away the protruding triangles ⅛" [4.5 mm] from the stitching line.

Trim ⅛" [4.5 mm] away from stitching.

4. Join the pieced border strips to the quilt center, measuring and pin matching as for "Mitered Corners" on page 75. Sew the seams, following the method for mitering corners. The point of the center half Nine Patch block should be in line with the point of the center setting triangle to make the zigzag effect around the quilt.

Quilting

1. Measure and cut two 8" [20 cm] strips from the backing fabric. Sew these two strips together end to end, and then sew the long strip to one side of the remaining background fabric to make the quilt backing. Trim square.

2. Layer the backing, batting, and quilt top, referring to "Layering" on page 78.

3. Baste the layers together, referring to "Pin Basting" on page 79 if you'll be machine quilting or "Thread Basting" on page 79 if you'll be hand quilting.

4. Quilt as desired. We suggest quilting in the ditch around the blocks and the squares within the Nine Patch blocks, outline quilting around all parts of the flowers, and meander quilting in the background of the appliqué blocks and setting triangles.

Finishing

Review "Binding" on page 90.

1. Cut one of the binding strips into four equal strips. Join these short strips to the remaining four strips.

2. Attach the binding to your quilt.

Appliqué patterns do not include seam allowances.

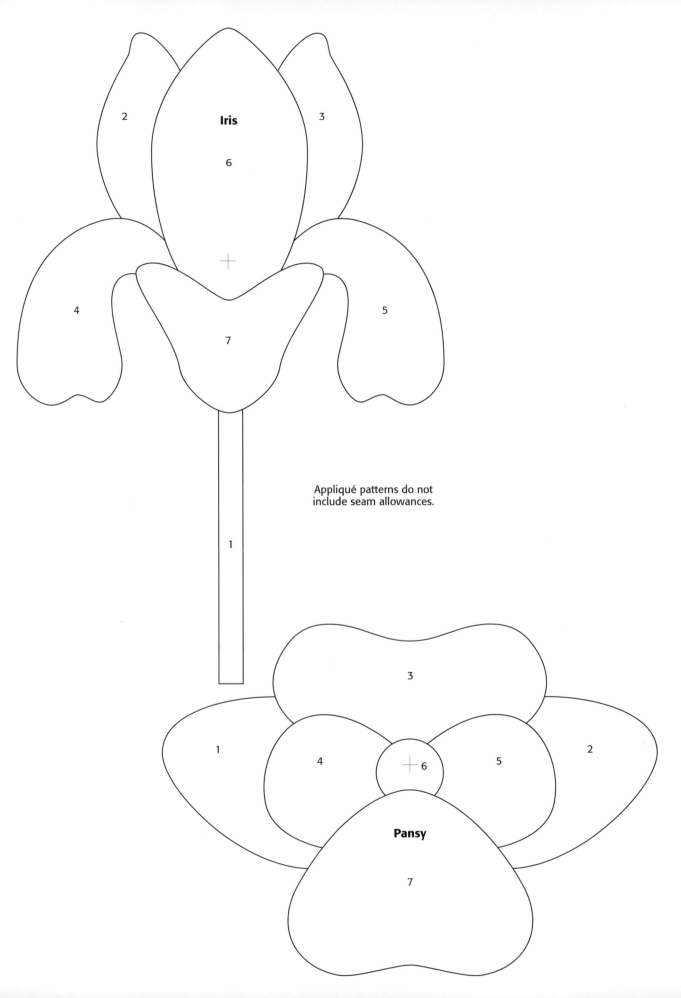

Iris

Appliqué patterns do not include seam allowances.

Pansy

SPRING FLIGHT by Jenny Bowker

Flying Geese give you an opportunity to showcase a wonderful large-scale border print or floral print fabric, as well as to mix and match other, smaller bits of fabrics in the Flying Geese themselves. We recommend that you choose your border or main print first and then select a variety of other prints and a background fabric to coordinate. Make sure that you have variety in the flying-geese prints to add interest. This style of quilt, with alternating strips of fabric and piecing, is called a "strippy" setting.

Size of quilt top: 62½" x 48½" [156 cm x 121.5 cm]
Flying-geese unit size: 6" x 3" [15 cm x 7.5 cm]

Flying Geese Unit

Materials

Amounts are based on 42" [106 cm]-wide fabric

- 2 yards [1.9 m] of background print or solid for flying-geese units, inner border, and binding
- 1½ yards [1.4 m] of large-scale print for strips and outer border
- Fat eighth or ⅛ yard [15 cm] of 8 assorted prints
- 3 yards [2.7 m] of backing fabric
- 66" x 52" [165 cm x 130 cm] piece of batting

Cutting

Cut across the width of the fabric, unless otherwise specified.

From the background fabric, cut:
- 6 strips, 2½" [7 cm] wide

From the lengthwise grain of the remaining background fabric, cut:
- 8 strips, 1½" [4 cm] wide
- 7 strips, 3½" [9 cm] wide; crosscut into 96 squares, 3½" x 3½" [9 cm x 9 cm]

From each of the 8 assorted prints, cut:
- 1 strip, 3½" [9 cm] wide (note: cut 2 strips per fabric if using fat eighths); crosscut into 6 rectangles, 3½" x 6½" [9 cm x 16.5 cm], to make 48 total

From the large-scale print, cut on the lengthwise grain:
- 6 strips, 6½" [16.5 cm] wide

Making the Flying-Geese Units

Using the 3½" x 6½" [9 cm x 16.5 cm] rectangles and the 3½" x 3½" [9 cm x 9 cm] background squares, make 48 flying-geese units, referring to "Flying Geese" on page 53.

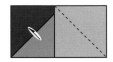 

Make 48.

Assembling the Quilt Center

1. Lay out the flying-geese units in vertical rows, mixing the prints and balancing the colors. Each row will have 16 units. Join the flying-geese units to make the rows. Press the seam allowances away from the points of the geese.

2. Lay out a flying-geese row in a clear space. Square up one end on each of six of the 1½" [4 cm]-wide background strips, and then measure the strips to the same length as the flying-geese row, referring to "Butted Corners" on page 73. Cut the six strips to this length

Make 3.

3. In the same manner, measure and trim two of the 6½" [16.5 cm] large-scale print strips to the same length.

4. Join a narrow strip of background fabric to each side of the flying-geese rows. Press the seam allowances toward the background strips.

5. Join the large-scale-print strips between the flying-geese rows. Press the seam allowances toward the large-scale-print strips.

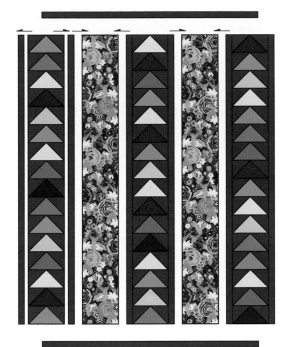

6. Lay out the quilt center. Square up one end each on the two remaining narrow background strips, and then lay the strips across the width of the quilt to determine the correct length. Cut the strips to this length, and join them to the top and bottom of the quilt.

Adding the Outer Border

1. Square up one end on each of two of the 6½" [16.5 cm] large-scale-print strips. Measure the strips to the length of the quilt, as you did for the background strips. Cut the strips to this length. Pin and sew them to the sides of the quilt. Press the seam allowances toward the borders.

2. Square up one end on each of the two remaining border strips. Measure the strips to the width of the quilt. Cut the strips to this length. Pin and sew them to the quilt top and bottom. Press the seam allowances toward the borders.

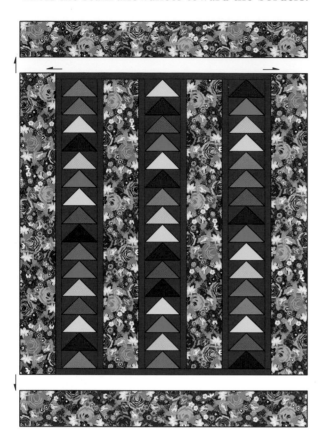

Quilting

1. Cut the backing fabric in half and join the two pieces side by side.

2. Layer the backing, batting, and quilt top, referring to "Layering" on page 78.

3. Baste the layers together, referring to "Pin Basting" on page 79 if you'll be machine quilting or "Thread Basting" on page 79 if you'll be hand quilting.

4. Quilt as desired. One suggestion is to outline quilt the flying geese, print strips, and borders, and then add further straight lines to the print strips and borders.

Finishing

Review "Binding" on page 90.

1. Cut a 12" [30 cm] length from each of two 2½" [7 cm]-wide binding strips. Join these short strips to two full-length strips. Join the remaining lengths to the two remaining full-length strips.

2. Attach the binding to your quilt.

Flying Geese Variation

Pretty blue prints contrast with white in this bed-size quilt. Eleven fat quarters of blue prints were used to make the 125 flying geese.

FLYING INTO THE BLUE by Margaret Rolfe

Leftovers from the Flying Geese

The leftover triangles from the flying-geese units make a charming small quilt when you assemble them into Broken Dishes blocks (see page 55). This quilt is 45" x 45" [115 cm x 115 cm]. You'll need an additional 1⅛ yards [1 m] of background fabric and ⅞ yard [90 cm] of border fabric, but in the end you'll have two quilts for hardly more than the price of one! It's important to trim your flying-geese units accurately if you want to use the leftovers.

LEFTOVERS ON BROKEN DISHES by Jenny Bowker

HARVEST GOLD by Jenny Bowker

This quilt is made just from squares and quarter-square triangles, creating a glowing star-within-a-star design. It uses only two fabrics; the key is that they contrast with each other to carry the design.

Size of quilt top: 40½" x 40½" [104.5 cm x 104.5 cm]
Finished block size: 9" [24 cm]

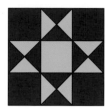

Ohio Star Block

Alternate Block

Materials

Amounts are based on 42" [106 cm]-wide fabric

- 1⅓ yards [1.2 m] of background fabric for stars, alternate blocks, and outer border
- 1 yard [1 m] of contrast fabric for stars, alternate blocks, inner border, and binding
- 1⅝ yards [1.5 m] of backing fabric
- 44" x 44" [113 cm x 113 cm] piece of batting

Cutting

Cut across the width of the fabric.

From the background fabric, cut:
- 1 strip, 10¼" [27.5 cm x 27.5 cm] wide; crosscut into 2 squares, 10¼" x 10¼" [27.5 cm x 27.5 cm]. From the remainder of the strip, cut 2 strips, 4¼" [11.5 cm] wide; crosscut into 8 squares, 4¼" x 4¼" [11.5 cm x 11.5 cm].
- 1 strip, 4¼" [11.5 cm] wide; crosscut into 2 squares, 4¼" x 4¼" [11.5 cm x 11.5 cm] (total 10 squares). Trim the remainder of the strip to 3½" [9.5 cm] wide.

- 1 strip, 3½" [9.5 cm] wide; from this and the other 3½" [9.5 cm]-wide strip, crosscut 17 squares, 3½" x 3½" [9.5 cm x 9.5 cm]
- 4 strips, 6" [14.5 cm] wide

From the contrast fabric, cut:
- 1 strip, 10¼" [27.5 cm x 27.5 cm] wide; crosscut into 2 squares, 10¼" x 10¼" [27.5 cm x 27.5 cm]. From the remainder of the strip, cut 2 strips, 4¼" [11.5 cm] wide; crosscut into 8 squares, 4¼" x 4¼" [11.5 cm x 11.5 cm].
- 1 strip, 4¼" [11.5 cm] wide; crosscut into 2 squares, 4¼" x 4¼" [11.5 cm x 11.5 cm] (total 10 squares). Trim the remainder of the strip to 3½" [9.5 cm] wide and crosscut into 8 squares, 3½" x 3½" [9.5 cm x 9.5 cm].
- 4 strips, 1½" [4 cm] wide
- 5 strips, 2½" [7 cm] wide

Making the Ohio Star and Alternate Blocks

1. Using the 10¼" [27.5 cm] squares of the background and contrast fabrics, make four 9" [24 cm] quarter-square triangle units, referring to "Piecing Quarter-Square-Triangle Units" on page 51.

Make 4.

2. Using the 4¼" [11.5 cm] squares of the background and contrast fabrics, make twenty 3" [8 cm] quarter-square-triangle units.

Make 20.

3. Lay out the 3½" [9.5 cm] squares and the small quarter-square-triangle units to make four Ohio Star blocks with the background fabric in the corners and the contrast fabric in the center. Also make one Ohio Star block with the contrast fabric in the corners and the background fabric in the center. Sew each of the blocks together and press the seam allowances toward the solid squares.

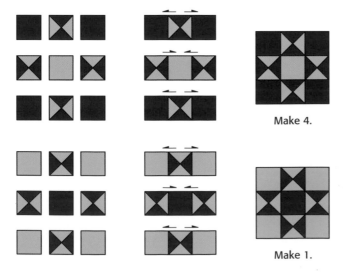

Make 4.

Make 1.

Assembling the Quilt

1. Lay out the blocks as shown. Join the blocks into rows, pressing the seam allowances toward the large quarter-square-triangle units.

2. Join the rows to complete the quilt center. Press.

Adding the Borders

1. Square up one end each on two of the 1½" [4 cm] contrast fabric inner-border strips. Measure the strips to fit the length of the quilt, referring to "Butted Corners" on page 73. Cut the strips to this length. Pin and sew them to the quilt sides.

2. Square up one end of each of the two remaining inner-border strips. Measure the strips to fit the width of the quilt, again referring to "Butted Corners." Cut the strips to this length. Pin and sew them to the top and bottom of the quilt. Press the seam allowances toward the border.

3. Measure and trim the 6" [14.5 cm]-wide main fabric outer-border strips, and add them to the quilt in the same manner as for the inner border.

Quilting

1. Measure and cut two 4½" [11.5 cm] strips from the backing fabric. Sew these two strips together end to end, and then sew the long strip to one side of the remaining background fabric to make the quilt backing. Trim square.

2. Layer the backing, batting, and quilt top, referring to "Layering" on page 78.

3. Baste the layers together, referring to "Pin Basting" on page 79 if you'll be machine quilting or "Thread Basting" on page 79 if you'll be hand quilting.

4. Quilt as desired. We suggest outline quilting star shapes and borders, and free-motion quilting spirals all over the quilt, matching thread colors to fabrics.

Finishing

Review "Binding" on page 90.

1. Cut one of the binding strips in half and join each half to a full-length strip.

2. Attach the binding to your quilt.

Ohio Star Variation

This quilt is an ideal holiday decoration for your own home or to give as a gift. The same print fabric was used for both the background and the binding.

CHRISTMAS STAR by Margaret Rolfe

Ready Guide to Cutting Sizes

CUTTING CHART FOR IMPERIAL MEASUREMENTS

Finished Size	□ **Add ½"**	⧄ **Add ⅞"**	⊠ **Add 1¼"**
½"	1"		
¾"	1¼"		
1"	1½"	1⅞"	2¼"
1¼"	1¾"	2⅛"	2½"
1½"	2"	2⅜"	2¾"
2"	2½"	2⅞"	3¼"
2¼"	2¾"	3⅛"	3½"
2½"	3"	3⅜"	3¾"
3"	3½"	3⅞"	4¼"
3½"	4"	4⅜"	4¾"
4"	4½"	4⅞"	5¼"
4½"	5"	5⅜"	5¾"
5"	5½"	5⅞"	6¼"
6"	6½"	6⅞"	7¼"
6½"	7"	7⅜"	7¾"
7"	7½"	7⅞"	8¼"
7½"	8"	8⅜"	8¾"
8"	8½"	8⅞"	9¼"
9"	9½"	9⅞"	10¼"
10"	10½"	10⅞"	11¼"
10½"	11"	11⅜"	11¾"
11"	11½"	11⅞"	12¼"
12"	12½"	12⅞"	13¼"
14"	14½"	14⅞"	15¼"
15"	15½"	15⅞"	16¼"
16"	16½"	16⅞"	17¼"
18"	18½"	18⅞"	19¼"
20"	20½"	20⅞"	21¼"

Ready Guide to Cutting Sizes

CUTTING CHART FOR METRIC MEASUREMENTS			
Finished Size	☐ **Add 1.5 cm**	◺ **Add 2.5 cm**	◿ **Add 3.5 cm**
1.5 cm	3 cm		
2 cm	3.5 cm		
2.5 cm	4 cm	5 cm	6 cm
3 cm	4.5 cm	5.5 cm	6.5 cm
4 cm	5.5 cm	6.5 cm	7.5 cm
5 cm	6.5 cm	7.5 cm	8.5 cm
6 cm	7.5 cm	8.5 cm	9.5 cm
7 cm	8.5 cm	9.5 cm	10.5 cm
8 cm	9.5 cm	10.5 cm	11.5 cm
9 cm	10.5 cm	11.5 cm	12.5 cm
10 cm	11.5 cm	12.5 cm	13.5 cm
12 cm	13.5 cm	14.5 cm	15.5 cm
14 cm	15.5 cm	16.5 cm	17.5 cm
15 cm	16.5 cm	17.5 cm	18.5 cm
16 cm	17.5 cm	18.5 cm	19.5 cm
18 cm	19.5 cm	20.5 cm	21.5 cm
21 cm	22.5 cm	23.5 cm	24.5 cm
22 cm	23.5 cm	24.5 cm	25.5 cm
24 cm	25.5 cm	26.5 cm	27.5 cm
27 cm	28.5 cm	29.5 cm	30.5 cm
28 cm	29.5 cm	30.5 cm	31.5 cm
30 cm	31.5 cm	32.5 cm	33.5 cm
32 cm	33.5 cm	34.5 cm	35.5 cm
36 cm	37.5 cm	38.5 cm	39.5 cm
40 cm	41.5 cm	42.5 cm	43.5 cm
48 cm	49.5 cm	50.5 cm	51.5 cm
50 cm	51.5 cm	52.5 cm	53.5 cm
60 cm	61.5 cm	62.5 cm	63.5 cm

Triangles are cut so that the outside is on the straight grain. Cut side triangles as quarter-square triangles (cut square into 4); cut corner triangles as half-square triangles (cut square into 2).

IMPERIAL MEASUREMENTS			METRIC MEASUREMENTS		
Finished Size of Block	Cut Size for Side Triangles ⊠	Cut Size for Corner Triangles ◺	Finished Size of Block	Cut Size for Side Triangles ⊠	Cut Size for Corner Triangles ◺
4"	7"	3¾"	10 cm	18 cm	10 cm
6"	9¾"	5⅛"	15 cm	25 cm	13.5 cm
7½"	11⅞"	6¼"	18 cm	29 cm	15.5 cm
8"	12⅝"	6⅝"	20 cm	32 cm	17 cm
9"	14"	7¼"	24 cm	37.5 cm	19.5 cm
12"	18¼"	9⅜"	30 cm	46 cm	24 cm

Index

About the Authors

Margaret Rolfe is an Australian quiltmaker and quilt book author. Her serious interest in quilts began while visiting Los Angeles during the summer of 1975, a time when Americans were rediscovering their rich heritage of quilts. At first she delightedly explored the traditional designs, and then later began to create her own original designs for blocks and quilts, especially quilts with animal themes. Her interest developed into a profession in the 1980s when she started to write quilt books and research the history of quilts in Australia.

Margaret's titles include *A Quilter's Ark*, *Animal Kingdom CD-ROM*, *Australian Quilt Heritage*, *Spectacular Scraps* (coauthored with Judy Hooworth), and *Successful Scrap Quilts* (coauthored with Judy Turner). Margaret has taught and lectured in Australia, New Zealand, Canada, the United Kingdom, France, and the United States. In 2001 Margaret was made a Member of the Order of Australia in recognition of her contribution to quiltmaking and the conservation of Australia's quilt heritage.

Margaret lives in Canberra with her scientist husband, Barry, and her dog and cat. Her two married sons and her daughter live in Melbourne.

Jenny Bowker is an Australian quiltmaker and quilting teacher. She doesn't remember a time when she didn't sew. She started her working career in science, but found it incompatible with her traveling way of life when she married a diplomat. She began to paint while living in countries such as Syria, Malaysia, and Jordan. As a mature student she completed a degree in Visual Art in 1997. She decided to make just one quilt to celebrate, and seven years later she is still making quilts. She began teaching in Jerusalem only one year after she started quilting, and she loves to teach. She has won three "Best of Show" awards in Australia, has been featured in *Quilter's Newsletter* magazine and many Australian magazines, and was nominated for Professional Quilt Teacher of the Year in 2003. She has recently returned from a trip to Ramallah where she taught a beginner's course to women who had never seen quilts before. She loves the process of teaching quiltmaking, as it is like giving women wings to fly.

Jenny lives in Canberra with her diplomat husband, her two younger children, and her chow and cat. She has two married daughters and five grandchildren.